Letters from Aldenderry

Born in Moscow in 1966 and raised in Russia and Moldova, Philip Nikolayev grew up equally fluent in English and Russian. On relocating to the US in 1990 to attend Harvard he has written primarily in English. His poetry is published internationally. Nikolayev's previous collections include *Monkey Time*, winner of the 2001 Verse Prize. He lives in Boston and co-edits *Fulcrum: an annual of poetry and aesthetics*.

Also by Philip Nikolayev

Poetry
  Monkey Time (Verse Press, 2003)
  Dusk Raga (Writers Workshop, 1998)
  Artery Lumen (Barbara Matteau Editions, 1996)

Letters from Aldenderry

PHILIP NIKOLAYEV

PUBLISHED BY SALT PUBLISHING
PO Box 937, Great Wilbraham, Cambridge PDO CB21 5JX United Kingdom

All rights reserved

© Philip Nikolayev, 2006

The right of Philip Nikolayev to be identified as the
author of this work has been asserted by him in accordance
with Section 77 of the Copyright, Designs and Patents Act 1988.

This book is in copyright. Subject to statutory exception
and to provisions of relevant collective licensing agreements,
no reproduction of any part may take place without the written
permission of Salt Publishing.

First published 2006

Printed and bound in the United Kingdom by Lightning Source

Typeset in Swift 9.5 / 13

This book is sold subject to the conditions that it shall not,
by way of trade or otherwise, be lent, re-sold, hired out,
or otherwise circulated without the publisher's prior consent
in any form of binding or cover other than that in which
it is published and without a similar condition including this
condition being imposed on the subsequent purchaser.

ISBN-13 978 1 84471 279 3 paperback
ISBN-10 1 84471 279 6 paperback

Salt Publishing Ltd gratefully acknowledges
the financial assistance of Arts Council England

1 3 5 7 9 8 6 4 2

Contents

Eagles	1
Secluded	2
Thunders	4
Pyromania	5
A Key in the Puddle	6
Locked	7
Nostalgia	8
You Who	9
The Art of Forgetting	10
A Plaint on the Parting of Inversion from Poetry	12
Were I Not	13
Old Hell	14
Title Disease	16
Still Communicating	19
The Green Square	20
Tendency toward Vagrancy	21
Grizzly	23
Green Eye	24
Apple Seeds	25
Good Enough	27
Lunch	28
Nightcap	30
On Falling Asleep in August Hot Wee Hours	31
A Secret Open Secret	33
A Fund of Hedge Funds	34
Eternal City	35
Not Otherwise Thought	37
Diotima's Lesson	38
Need to Talk	39

Hymn	40
Moi aussi j'aime les nuages qui passent là-bas	41
Odessa Herring 1983	42
Seeing	43
Stargazing	44
Discipline	45
A Stately Goodbye	46
For Stephen Sturgeon	47
"Things happen as if not happening . . ."	48
Hold that Thought	49
Unhappening	50
Morning	51
Facts of Life	52
"these pages turn cold in the wind . . ."	53
"In this vat of wishful hearts . . ."	54
Revolution	55
Homage to Paradox	57
Cicadas	59
Book Tongue	60
"My name is Wormswurst, I give back to men their Zen . . ."	61
Hotel	62
Sharks	63
Life	64
The Next Level	65
"I wish to live my life like a house insect . . ."	66
"Global bacteria local euphoria . . ."	67
Folklore	68
Urbane Suburbia	69
A Quarry of Words	70
19 March 2004	71
Crocodile	72

Farewell	73
A Midsummer Night's Stroll	74
A Ghazal	77
Commencement Walk	78
I Am not Used to Using a Cell Phone	79
Poetry Month Poem	80
Rhetoric	81
Target Practice	82
The Cure	83
The Seeded Friend of Humankind Is Cashed	84
The Nut Club	85
Zeno's Stoop	86
Offer	87
Ideers	88
A Letter to the Antipodes	90
Pensées	91
Ithinkistillcanhear	93
Ideas	94
"A taste that loves the classical cliché . . ."	95
Benares USA	96
In a Hospital	97
Nothing Changes	99
Philosophy & Rhetoric	100
One Sensation, Two Sensation	101
I'll Write	102
Coastwise Lights	103
Suburbi Et Suborbi	104
Recollections	105
To Assuage	106
States of Affairs	107
A Silence within a Silence	108

Simple Joys of Food & Drink	109
Letters from the Past	110
Indian Summer	111
Modulo Feeling	112
Litmus Test	114
"God, empowered to the max . . ."	117
A Life, in 500 Words or Less	118
Earth	122

Acknowledgements

The author wishes to acknowledge the editors of the following publications, in which some of these poems have previously appeared, occasionally in a substantially different version: "Locked" in *The Boston Globe*; "Nostalgia," The Green Square," "Good Enough" in *Harvard Review*; "Litmus Test" in *Jacket*; "Diotima's Lesson," "In a Hospital" in the *Journal of Postcolonial Writing*; "Pyromania," "A Fund of Hedge Funds" in *LIT*; "Snow," "A Midsummer's Night Stroll," "Ideers" in *Mirage Periodical*; "Odessa Herring 1983," "The Seeded Friend of Humankind is Cashed," "Seeing," "Stargazing" in *Rattapallax*, "Coastwise Lights" in *Salamander*.

Several of the poems in this collection were published in the chapbook, *5 Poems* (A Rest Press, New York, 2005).

Eagles

Two eagles circled over Cambridge today,
a rare sight, lovely
against the chalkboard sky.
Drawn to stare, I soon noticed
that they went around in near perfect circles
at even speed.
In fact they looked exactly identical.
Their widespread wings didn't so much as flutter.
I heard a thin electrical whiz
and wondered if they carried
tiny surveillance cameras on board
that could scan
"Shakespeare and the Pathos of Rambling" that I was reading.

Secluded

The water truck is stuck,
a callow yellow mushroom
marshmallow, among branches tangled
with birdships and their nests,
with bishoprics of twitter.
I am into the kitchen garden,
primroses of the gods creep up my sleeves,
extend out the situation.
Whatever falls into the eye falls.
You can't open the same door twice,
you can barely open it once,
and then you find yourself silhouetted
all out of proportion against the
duration of their fall down the cast iron grille
of the kitchen garden.
Morning exercises of the will,
nicotine, attempts at staying afloat,
if not on top of things. Whatever
is the water truck doing here,
what stitches it in this fabric?
Throughout the fall they fall,
while there is indeed a run, what the British call
a ladder. Thus the need for a mender.
Ah to have been sequentially estranged,
by attrition rather than ambition,
into such a loophole of oneself, such a
snail's carapace of self
in the material garden of things,
that exit were temporarily precluded.
Maybe that's why the water truck is here,
and it's time someone answered the phone:
its ringing pierces
the stuffed owl to the bone,

me to pieces. Alone,
I'm into the kitchen
garden. Under turn-key.
Secluded zone.

Thunders

1.

Throughout the musicolored sky
and visible land —
swift alternation of night and day
with more blinding crashes
per minute per minute per minute.
Tonight they really mean it up there
and are gonna make a big racket
for fully a couple of hours
across rain hanging in strobe tatters.
Car alarms go off in the thunder
and the photosensitive lighting of the parking lot
keeps coming on and off and on and off,
weakling competitor to the sky.
All windows stay fast unlit. Electricity
wells, smells and clangs a thousands bells.
In the middle of this mess,
absolutely and temporarily free,
a poet on the balcony
smokes into the sky,
grateful that he couldn't sleep.

2.

At the playground with Sophia at 6:30 p.m.,
an F15 fighter jet flew by low
(nowadays they sometimes do that on purpose)
sending off a shockwave of sound and fury through the streets,
triggering car alarms at the said parking lot.
Once the air-blast passed,
the playground filled with the weaker
alarms of stunned children,
the sandbox sounding the most desperate.

Pyromania

Whatever happened to the childproof lighter?
I don't see them on counters any more,
but I remember that day in 1995
that I bought my first
(since Nini's Corner didn't carry the normal kind)
and on a midnight subway ride
across Boston tried
to figure out how to use it,
but couldn't. The sticker
read in terse verse:
To operate push
button in and up,
rotate sparkwheel,
push down on lever.
But I saw no button. The sparkwheel
kept firing into the void until eventually
a heavily stoned good natured fellow from across
the aisle volunteered to help me. He said,
hey I done seen this shit before lemme try
and pointed out the safety button, cached shyly
on the back of the activation lever,
then asked if I had a pen on me.
Surprised but professional, I produced a pen
and he used the ballpoint expertly
to pry and rip out the disabling button.
Try it now, he said. I did. The damn thing
exploded in our face, singing our eyebrows.

A Key in the Puddle

At the foot of the Caucasus on the Black Sea
in Sochi, they stood me under palms when I was three
in my red shorts and mom told me
not to screw up my eyes against the sun,
but I couldn't help it. I still screw them up
because the sun's too bright and the photographer
chuckles, making me uneasy. I came out
slit-eyed with sun-bleached hair
under the palms and with the facial features of
vaguely Ugro-Finnic physical anthropology.
There are fat miller's thumbs aplenty
in the clear Khosta river, though the hook
frequently gets stuck against bottom snags.
My newspaper hat sails away toward the Black Sea.
I've made acquaintance with shy lizards
of the boxwood grove. My pet female mantis
prays as she devours her puny husband
in my sand bucket. Then I see
a lost apartment key
in a sunny puddle on a wish-filled walk after some rain.
I say, "Dad, look." He looks.
"Ho-ho-ho, so have you found
the key to your life, maybe, or, as they say,
the key to the money-stuffed apartment?"—
"Yes!" say I, laughing, though I've no idea.

Locked

I know two homeless men, they both believe
that evil forces have messed with their lives.
Always, every time something good seemed about to happen,
something really bad happened,
and so it keeps going on
for ever and ever more—
like a bad spell, a curse.
Evil forces will do anything,
repeatedly steal your eyeglasses to keep you from reading,
put you in trouble with the law,
cut the strings of your guitar, plagiarize your songs,
gun down your mother in a Chicago supermarket
during a late night shift (this a long time ago),
make you sleep God knows where, God knows how, alone.
Whenever there's the littlest chance of a romance,
some nasty shit happens and screws it all to bits.
One believes in an afterlife and in numerology,
the other is an atheist but sings in a church.
If you carry a guitar the cops don't harass you as much.
If you panhandle and get donations from college students,
cops will suspect you're pushing dime bags.
They both hate the distant, indifferent rich
and both respect me just because I'm a poet.
How locked are we all into our respective fates.
The rich can't help being rich, the poor poor,
the invisible hand piles invisible cash,
wants its streets clean of trash.

Nostalgia

Good thing we no longer write poems about
a Red Skimmer dragonfly alighting on a poem,
ignoring the true autobiographical fact—
nor about anything good that we have done.
Autobiography no longer saves.
The old masters, they
savored every comprimé of pain & painkiller:
it near killed all of them,
with the exception of those that it killed.
They died the death of unfulfilled nostalgia.
Now we have innovation,
a novel preciousness & pride, a fresh method
of feeling good or at least better about ourselves.
It too no longer saves,
but it no longer kills us either,
does it?

You Who

You, savage Sicilian Irish,
the sharpest string in our Beethoven quartet,
who kick butt long distance but drive
three hours so we can compare our spondees
and fill up right and proper with Blue Moon,
you who then drive
us all who can't drive
back another three into your woods
(man, I abhor your techno selections),
you who bring out two power fans
against the mosquitoes
so we can while away the stars in open air,
you who make Amherst inhabited,
who when a fellow insulted me yelled
in the best accent of your youth
I'll serve his ass some Jersey justice
with meaning and purpose,
who cook fine French dinners for your dog,
you, lunatic prepostmodern Catholic,
who call on Christmas at midnight
us, who trashed our blinking lights two years ago,
you who yell merrily
Hi! It's John Hennessy! Are you guys celebrating?
who rouse me out of my oblivion,
who make sparks fly where there were none,
must you always announce yourself,
do you think I have forgotten your voice?

The Art of Forgetting

Last night I cooked my socks in the microwave
by mistake. What to do when you're so absent
minded? As well, I have frequently
refrigerated my poems in the freezer
to the point of having to thaw them later,
and poetry's what's emerges in defrosting.
I have also lost to nature generations
of galoshes, coats, scarves, umbrellas,
even once an Egyptian skullcap,
whose individual names I forget.
The name of the czar escapes my mind
on whom was meant to be my dissertation,
or was it thesis. Water,
all kinds of water under the all-purpose bridge.
If I've forgotten so much via absentmindedness mostly,
then how much have we forgotten as a species?
One day we learn, another forget
everything, including this fact.
It's possible given enough time and effort
to forget anything,
which's why we like to reminisce sometimes
on those even who've decided they don't like us.
We'll *fight* for our memories, the truth as it appeared once.
But to remember something we need to forget
something, a different truth. My grandmother
believed that if you dab any convenient spot on your body
with iodine daily
it will help you keep your memory in old age.
Head of the Marxism-Leninism chair
at the Ivanovo Energy Institute,
where she taught philosophy and scientific atheism,
she was the kindest soul, loved and spoiled me to distraction,
and her blueberry cakes were of course the best
in this world. Baptized as a child,
on her retirement to a small apartment in the Crimea

she read the Bible, perestroika raging all around.
Everyone wrote, thought and talked of
Stalin, Stalin, Stalin, Beria, Stalin.
She read the Bible, both the Testaments.
Thus dialectical materialism was forgotten
and an ancient faith recovered.
I too would like to forget a few things,
keep trying, but tend to forget instead
all the wrong ones, like submitting payments
by the due date, the need to tie my shoestrings.
Mnemosyne, and her daughters the Muses,
and her grandsons the museums . . .
Literature too is a museum,
as well as Lenin's mausoleum,
which is essentially a tomb.
As you must of course know I've forgotten
the remote control on the bathroom sink
where my reflection in the crooked mirror
distracted me with its scowl.
This is earth life, but like hailing from outer space.
When my daughter was born,
I spent the night with her and my wife at the hospital
and went home the next day to clean the apartment.
I vacuumed the floor very thoroughly,
my thoughts soaring far and wide. Little did I notice
that the vacuum was running in blow out mode
so the condition of the floor changed
hardly at all. This still makes my wife laugh
and may indeed be worth remembering
against all death. While stress, duress and strain,
the painful neck crane
and other stuff rotten
are best forgotten.

A Plaint on the Parting of Inversion from Poetry

Impossible's inversion, say they —
therewith to differ beg I please may!

To clarify sometimes used it's,
as verify help you your wits.

Invert everything and you'll see,
and see'll you everything invert.

Like today blossom you a tree,
but dust tomorrow are and dirt.

Becometh every gem a sand,
still but try we to understand

laws mandatory what prevail,
what from what follows without fail.

Why indeed not, indeed not why
on life get drunk we before die.

Nature's melancholy in humors,
ourself expunge from earthy rumors

and crux into the formal dig,
back in put poetry a wig

bitter and face the boldly sand,
better so can we understand.

Friend, doing out there are you how?
Me understand you better now?

Let together then us perform
inversion formal of the norm.

Were I Not

Sometimes, crystalline clear our prism of comprehension,
we proceed to think with innocent intention
of the touchable world that it's open to cognition
and go on to tease out the sources of its ignition.

But all yesterday I spent on my bed, half reading,
more reflecting on nothing with such lethargic focus,
that the loins of reality shed their fancy girding
and its naked premises lay fundamentally bogus

and the soul was again the prison-house of the body
(as a manner of speaking or rather of not speaking)
while the surface of logic moved ruddy, if not bloody,
with its governed transitions however cleanly squeaking.

Then I fell asleep in a sense of pervasive hollow,
would be Buddha were I not Philip Nikolayev.
In the light of dreams I might have become Apollo,
but did not because I lacked the internal drive.

Old Hell

The other night I visited Old Hell. Hell used to be here
before they moved it to the New place. Old Hell
is now more of a museum or a visiting space.
It is a mound or mount the size of Hollywood
with the structure of a macro anthill,
built through internally with a mammoth scheme of corridors,
rooms, passages, shafts, stairwells straight and spiral,
and standalone stairs. Some have built-in music but it uses
another time and is unintelligible: *a music not for us.*
One staircase, only six flights to the top, took me a while.
There were signals you knew were there—
thought you could not see them, could not not see them,
knowing they could see you. The mind-
boggling web of continual shifting transitions,
locations, defined reference, refined deference points
with solid pale doors, stray volutes, mines
and nested colonnades, spills out onto the roof.
This is the surface part of Old Hell's township.
Like any old city, it boasts intricate lanes,
wells, haute chimneys and valved crossings,
inverted bridges, slant balconies, fireproof isles
and countless historic buildings to visit.
They keep forever changing. I was looking into a lens,
wondering if I should go in there and what I would find.
Some guests were walking slowly in the glazed compartments.
I left my family walking with them
and headed outside though a hatch,
intent on returning before long. The street was sadly uncrowded.
I could clearly see the corner where my man was standing,
seasonally employed, unshaven and homeless. I asked him,
"Whudcha got?" And he, "Anything, you name it,"
pulling from inside his coat end a page-long list
of mesmeric wonders. I didn't want them. "Whodja need?
World sponge?" I nod, perplexed at what hell he means.
"Oh that," he turns as if aloof, staring through and above me.

"I don't have that. But a lot of people go there ... "
He points into a side alley tending uphill,
two obscure pedestrians now receding through its gate.
I follow for a while, then suddenly notice the road is empty,
its black trees and houses mostly grown into the ground.
There isn't a soul. I have come quite a ways up the hill,
the rise has gotten steep.
Nobody really "goes here," I think.
I want to go and find my daughter and I look back,
but the road I have come along has changed.
I can see a big puddle of lead colored water
with cyan internal glow
staring upward at me attentively with gelid eyes
at the foot of the cracked road.
The puddle begins to crawl uphill,
up the slope, slowly at first, then faster, then in a swift stretch,
with intermittent pauses,
spreading itself forth in oblong spurts of tentacular tongues.
I, filled with a surge of violent defiance
and screaming "Dry up!" at the top of my lungs,
set off running downhill with all my might
toward the silently rushing puddle. In seconds
my heels crash through its dead fluttering face.

Title Disease
For Ben Mazer

Titles, titles turning trite
in mahoganies of night,
what abstemious hand has warped
your oblate avoirdupois?

Titles, I could use them all,
the oblique, elliptical,
and the plain, straightforward,
both my own and borrowed

by myself from me
(*The Dromedary's Diary!*)
those of pedant irony
(*The Philosophy Dictionary!*)

those traditional in style
(*Anna the Sailor!*)
or those bohemian by the mile
(*My Manual for Failure!*)

in any old idiolect
or centrally located,
titles that catch you in the act,
that make you elated!

Incubated,
by the author of the present recollection,
or,
How I Acted on the Eve of the Presidential Election!

You see, it's impossible to improvise
in rhyming verse,
nor write in a free personal style
like Williams or W C Williams.

Notice how "form" constricts my seat?
So, yeah, about titles. Need to eat
and dream that I could sell them all,
each for a dollar.

The Cambridge Misconstruing Company!
The Mills of the Verbooks!
Digital Digitalis!
The Philosophy Dictionary!

No, wish I could turn them off,
those ghosts of wood-be books,
but they keep popping up and up,
unable to stop.

A Few Slatternly Verses
on Criticism
that Are Gonna Destroy
Literary Criticism!

They casually occur,
sneak up with furtive ease.
Show me the drug that frees
the mind of this disease.

The Best Tested Hypothesis!
The Poet's Mind in Furs!
A Chapbook of Chapbook Titles!
(forerunner for a prize)

Just Justice! Unscrambled Eggs!
(quick, call Faber & Faber,
I'm going into labor)
The Emperor's Last Legs!

Their own artform,
titles, titles,
where do they come from?
Nobody knows.

Still Communicating

segmented sequestration felt deeply by the body cellular
we're still communicating even when all communications
fair fail when power dies in the switch the piano's
keys cave in completely especially the black ones
when the lights walk out of the cinema
the turns and tunes of tones immortal overtures
until the screen exploded like a huge popcorn
bomb and now you're inside it in the movie and in it's dark
the soundtrack is saying everything
except for your own lines
but language itself has evolved so far
it's not easy to comprehend for example where it means

Styrofoam deck declensions stabilize honorific
control flow with output or without privileging
motorcars over sense dance over
carpentry the goblets in the
dishwasher alabaster suffused with purple
vines of euphony and light just
enlightenment wet communication
entanglement with vintages of the voice

it actually says

glare at your own reflection with aversion
as it traipses out of the mirror
grates on the gates disintegrates

and those are your opening lines in fact
into the phone in the movie

The Green Square

Framed with timbers primeval,
Malevich's green square is an alfalfa field
with two diagonal deer and a third,
their young, at a slight angle to them
and looking aside, while his parents
stare at you most attentively,
white tails ready to budge
at first sign of danger—
eye contact with another civilization.

A power pole emphatic at center,
the power-line perpendicular,
and there's also this idea of speed,
of parallelism, a solid working model.
The occasional sand wasp
digs forth depths of orange dirt.

Haystacks are formidably cylindric.
A small tractor was rooting here yesterday,
followed around by a Yorkshire Terrier:
locals have taste. Another hayrick
a hemispherical anthill spied through tall grass.
Those three half-shaded beehives are Malevich,
followed by boulder wall.

Art works suprematism upon nature,
hoists platonic parabolas into barnyard,
industrializes the old triangular self,
still woven through with cones of dragonflies.

Tendency toward Vagrancy

I've long had what Soviet psychiatrists
called "a tendency toward vagrancy."
At four I would run away from home
repeatedly for a whole day, alone
or sometimes with a friend named Boris
of like age. Knew full well we "just can't do this,"
but nudge for nudge and wink for wink,
we'd board the trolleybus #10, I think,
buy tickets at four kopeks each
from our gleanings and savings of the week,
stick them into the ticket punch on the wall,
watch the chad fall as you pulled,
and ride all across Kishinev in half an hour
to get off near that unforgettable restaurant
built in the likeness of a huge wine barrel.
We peered inside, it was cool.

Then we had options:
go and splash in the local artificial lake
(I couldn't swim yet),
wonder in between along the banks,
catching frogs to take home in a glass jar
to populate a small construction pond (why
did we always use *my* shirt to do this?),
or go and explore the local flea market,
which was not at all safe to do,
but even at four it's nice to have options.
(One guy sold what we thought was a gun,
we asked him and he confirmed it.)

Those were days of cholera epidemics
in Moldova. We'd buy peasant-cooked
fodder corn on the cob when we got hungry,
haggled with old ladies over pennies.
We wouldn't catch the return trolley until sunset.

Then it's always the same picture:
the wicket creaks open, the landlord's mutant
barks through froth, my wet shirt clings,
I step out of the dark
toward my mother waiting by the door
of our "temporary house" on Kaluga Street,
which was a bit of a dirt road, probably still is.
She has been crying, takes me inside.

Room and kitchen (no bathroom
or running water); the room
had a brick stove, the kitchen
a dirt floor (with mice and sometimes grass)
and a white washstand—these lines
are all that has survived of them.
There was great beauty in their squalor.

She has been crying, takes me inside,
says she will scold me later.
I know it will be soon. First she must call
the cops to tell them I've been found.

Of course, back then I didn't understand anything:
neither how a poet harms his mother,
nor how alienated (thank you, Marx, for that term)
one can be from the start, and free
in the grip of that greatest paradox of all—
a happy Soviet childhood.

Grizzly

Every time I spill
coffee all over my project,
extinguish my cigarette in the watermelon
or accidentally kick the wastebasket
across our tiny home office,
the wife calls me "my Russian grizzly."
This is probably because I have
a rather concave face,
high-humped shoulders
and long, curved claws,
and also because
my weight varies widely
in the course of the year.
Too because I am
seasonally employed and
regularly in hibernation.
They say if you're going to be a bear,
be a grizzly, but that's because
people want respect and grizzlies get
respect. When pissed off,
grizzlies can be very fast,
especially if they are hungry.
I love the sound of the name
and everything that is grizzly,
but I haven't eaten
since morning
and am already beginning to not
like my own temper.
In five minutes
I severely dislike it. Another five
and I'm downright pissed off at myself.
No wonder I am an endangered species.

Green Eye

For one who's traveled far and wide, the strangest place is all inside. No statistic will aforetaste or know my path to yon place as I alone come to visit. For instance, my deep name ain't Jimmy Turnflower, I squish the will to power, let it die. ***nor Catherine Lyverwater, nor*** I too have stared back into Nietzsche's eye, ***Charles Cynthia Brown.*** but I've got little of the will to power ***It is rather . . . but no I won't say.*** (except to trick you with my words when I ***A thing that can peer into*** pluck out that mental landscape flower by flower), ***itself, like the pro*** and likewise I've conversed with Schopenhauer ***microscope my classmate*** (who slept nights with a firearm by his head ***Sheremetyev stole for me for*** and probably talked to himself in bed) ***my 14th b-day, which to this day*** of mouthless moths, short-lived—I have diffused ***stares into my brain*** the penchant of the will to self-devour, ***through my right eye, supposedly*** though I was moved, exercised and amused, ***making my gray cells grow,*** lost in the sudden weeness of the hour, ***to find there revolutionary names*** by their gravamens to my heart's content, ***and objects. I also recollect*** and thus consider those wee hours well spent. ***an earlier radio set with a green eye, how it was staring deep inside me. All those wavelengths marked Paris, London and Lisbon and so on, all false, what you heard was Soviet stations, and they explained to me Leonid Ilyich Brezhnev.***

Apple Seeds

I since childhood obsessively
eat the insides of apple seeds
after the apple itself.
Their bittery evanescence induces
thoughts. By reason of possible
residual levels of cyanide, ingesting
apple seeds is generally discouraged.
Cyanide's awful for you.
One marvels especially
at Mithridates VI of Pontus
(132–63 BC),
also known as Eupator Dionysius, a king
possessed of a prodigious memory,
prodigious bodily force
and prodigious cruelty, who knew
all soldiers by name of his monster army,
spoke twenty five languages, married
his sister and several other women, worried
some Roman ass in a few wars and had
far-reaching plans. Being like any
rational ruler scared of poisoning,
he would harden himself against its prospects
by taking homeopathic quantities
of the known venoms. When he finally
lost battle to General Pompey ("the Great")
and was betrayed by his own conspiring son,
Mithridates, to thwart capture by Rome,
poisoned his wives and daughters first and then
propelled the same concoction
down his own throat, but his earlier antidotal
electuaries proved extremely effective
against that, and so he actually had to pierce himself to die
by his own sword. This happened on Mithridates Hill

in the Crimea, where I paced a few times as a child,
with no doubt an apple in hand. Cicero calls Mithridates
"the greatest ruler who ever challenged Rome."
I am ambitious too
and sometimes wonder vaguely if my apple
seed crunching habits
have similarly antidoted me as much,
though I can't truly say I hope one day
to find out.

Good Enough

The ivory tower had a garbage chute. Down
I went smoothly, silently,
albeit the pages of my dissertation —

both written and half-written and unwritten —

a kind of reconstruction of the reign
of Grand Prince Boris Fyodorovich Godunov —

with whom I'd fallen strictly out of love
and favor,
fixated on writing something else instead

— fluttered and rustled distinctly for an hour.

All for the best, but anyone who's fed
a few quires to a garbage chute
retains for a while that sound.

                                  Am now
admiring yolks of water lilies on the sunny-
I'm-here-for-money-
side-up of this Concord corporate pond.

Ours is a season of abrupt transitions
and sundry melancholy dispositions,

but man forever conquers office space,
needing a job until such time
as he decide to lose it.

Lunch

A tin plate on a pine
advises against trespassing, but I
cross the rail tracks & trespass anyway,
hungry guy
angry on an empty stomach.

A groundhog
(some people call them "whistle pigs" regionally)
darts from the human path into the woods,
its broad flat head & short bushy tail
whoosh clear out of sight

as I advance over fresh-fallen fall yellows.

My office is behind those trees
in a flat one storey building—
small cubicle of hatred & hope,
elegant integration schemas
& business copy.

Hired angst goes grave,
but not so much at gravy hour.

A steak of salmon, a slice of lemon,
newspaper & small talk
with a Russian ex-mathematician
now in middle management.

Lighting a smoke to walk it all off
on the way back alone,
my brain activity submerges, turns internal,
goes to areas unrecountable
as I take a lengthy detour

all the way up to the Concord Prison
& then along an overgrown abandoned
rail track in soporific woods,
trusting the exercise to deliver its goods,

not noticing much of anything this time.

Nightcap

Wierdy doody dandy,
fix me a tall brandy,

a thermonucleozoroastrian
uninhibit of backbite,

intrafledgement of foxwit.
What to do with it?

Squander it on rigmaroles?
Pour it out in liquid forms in verse?

But days sail by, all draped in crap.
Each one calls for a nightcap.

Outlandish, stash me a bottle of equilibrium
somewhere under the pillow, a refill.

I'll drain it dry! Yep.

Thanks, kindly chap.

On Falling Asleep in August Hot Wee Hours

    1.

With diminishing bias psychological science offers greater
    reliance.
We prefer to dull waiters whereof we are patrons shrinks to whom
    we are clients.

With this cardiovascular mess and our eschatological guesswork
    adore to trace
all along this path in spacetime unstraight unnarrow down which
    we traipse.

In all manner of garb welcome in every manner of talented fuckup
but stay cool in reminding your boss that you're due for a markup.

If you leave it up to him to pay you a fair good rate
judged soberly it means you'll probably never get quite properly
    paid.

Your boss may well pretend to be your friend,
for bosses can do nothing but pretend.

Evolution happens every day, incidentally.
Between life and death we change a 100%.

2.

Tickers tick and factors rock,
acres populate the stock,
and the owners of this wood
must be up to not much good.

In untidy dreamy halls
duty calls like nature calls,
through the kitchen window falls
to the ground and breaks its balls.

But the tinkling by the lake
shakes no drifter soul awake.
Being blind, twined and asleep,
I have no promises to keep.

A Secret Open Secret

If you have a car you need to park it.
Therefore, parking also is a market.
I'm no senator or parakeet,
when you hear my word you'd better mark it.
You conceive a thought and want to birth it.
In addition you also need money.
Voluntary slavery is worth it.
Capitalism ain't remotely funny.
Organize your act in such a fashion
as to earn yourself a legal pension,
lest you merit eternal damnation
or at least a temporal suspension,
or come to a silly melodrama,
having trouble dealing with your feelings.
Double-billing isn't a misnomer
when your whiskey snifter needs refillings.
Everything's a need and a fulfillment.
Understand this and you'll win your battles
and deservedly receive in payment
a few handfuls of expensive metals.

So, can I open you a secret?
This way or that,
one must gnaw oneself out a
cubicle
in a world of precious sinecures.
I don't use the term lightly,
nor in any sort of derogatory sense,
but as the sole warrant of our cheap
survival.

If you have a talent then unearth it,
if you've got an idea then birth it.

A Fund of Hedge Funds

A Microsoft LiveMeeting on my computer is in progress.
Comment ça va? The guy in Paris
guides me through a thousand clicks
of financial risk simulation. Extreme betas
have plugged my ears, I can't listen
any more, so I tune out,
counting on my subconscious to do the work,
to emit ahhh when your fund of hedge funds
still shows a profit under certain stress-testing hypotheses,
exposed to the conditions of a historical crisis.
Vous comprenez bien cette fonctionalité?
Bah ouais mais bien sûr,
I eat, am and shit this functionality. Cuz when exposure—
clearly visualized on the blue spider chart
(financial color schemas must be aesthetically pleasing)—
reveals a longish leg along the corresponding factor axis, Equity,
we say we have identified our suspect by drilldown:
the distressed hedge fund, code withheld
for reasons of proprietary info confidentiality,
that is playing heavily on Equity.
Under full transparency we see the underlying positions
chez notre fund manager. Financial risk is interesting,
because ultimately risk indicators are non-additive.
I even wish I owned a fund of hedge funds,
or rather, screens flicking,
input parameters now turning negative,
I wish I could fall asleep this second,
dream that I'm walking down Wall Street,
my brain pockets full of plastic.

Eternal City
For Samuel Gareginyan

He who says that in art
one finds not the object
but its myth, himself stands
monastically thin
and looks like his own
self-portrait, the same eye
staring out at you,
marking your silhouette
against the wall or posture at table
with its wild precision.
He needs so few things that he got rid
of the chairs in his studio for want of space
and stands for hours as he finishes
Dionysus' hairy thigh
or the nymph's coy hand,
still on the hefty shoulder.
When out of his window
in war-torn Armenia
he gazed at the ruins
of Erevan's tall gardens
reduced to firewood,
he understood that to revive a place
one must by an effort of the soul
rebuild it from scratch, so he painted
his Eternal City
over three years in several apartments,
first there then here, and I
am now bound to roam it forever,
a myth impossible to exit.
When he went to real Rome,
he didn't like it,
although he did shudder
at the sight of aesthetic treasures
long photographed by his heart
to the obscurest detail.

He says there was too much food
and it was too good,
a distraction for the mind,
which must be hungry.
A feast once in a while is OK,
but Europe doesn't need any
more beauty: now an artist can live
only in America.

Not Otherwise Thought

The character whose sleep is messed up,
who is awakened by the least misstep
in a dream and hobbles to the stairwell to smoke,
can't quit however hard tried,
smoking on the landing on an empty stomach
does give consolation
as well as thoughts not otherwise thought,
leading upward and downward like the stripes we call stairs
with light bulbs so yellow
one can't tell whether the walls are beige or white,
never seen in plain day, who could be you
except that it may be me, dissolves instant coffee
in hot tap water in a pre-cracked cup, melts therein with sugar
all secondary considerations regarding awakening
his company of companions still
dormant, and who must slink quietly in the dark,
make an effort to breathe softly,
think peaceable thoughts lest an abrupt sound erupt,
rather glare at the obtruding moon for a time,
then back to the stairwell with your coffee,
with my cigarettes, to think some more thoughts
not otherwise thought,
the character whose sleep is all messed up.

Diotima's Lesson

There's Eros in the air, Mediterranean Eros that makes you high.
Spells of Eros, froth. The heart throbs out of the chest and bees
hunt down street nectars. You, whose hand appears to pluck pears
These flitting silver moths are evening's eyes "off of" pear trees
dancing their vigil round the lilac bush. of poetry. Then our well
Summer's intoxication makes us wise. studied smoke with mock
The god of passion grants our every wish. cruelties edged side-
The village sighs goodnights. Since vineyard toil ways into our
came to its restful pause, domestic lamps facial features. They
still hold desire but have spent all their oil. soon melt, become
What's that to us? Our fingers and our lips small tournaments
have miles to go yet before we get home of lips, turns to storms
with a few foolish fireflies in our hair. of eyelash gesture. Yes,
Are we immortal? Evanescent hope I do capitulate. Embrace me
spins lunar sweep-nets in the swooning air, coldly, dizzily, drive
and this experience fits like a glove deeply out all my sorrows,
what Diotima taught us about love. for I truly am going crazy
for the love of you. What do we do, where do we henceforth flee?
To the wee, the even downright minuscule room still available in
the motel—a single-bed with a view to finish what we promised.

Need to Talk
For Jeet Thayil

Moscow, provider and incineration box of hope, your tall streetlights are afflicted, your valerian drops dissolved, trams rattled on icy rails, steams wrapped into zero rings with dour infinities, cleaned up central streets aglitter, your drained out yard **Sad sitters in cafés, the milkfoam reapers,** puddles a-dry, your Paris-styled florist **knowers-keepers of Sunday's morning cream,** and expert dentist with their Cyprus-**waiters in windows for something seldom seen:** extended tan, pensionary poverty, **a stretch of sky to brighten up their peepers.** industry, dying and reborn and dying, **You, both the referent and that which refers,** your night life boxed into flower by **a fragment likewise struggling to get buy—** legal enterprise, two thirds of which are **I feel your sadness and would tell you why,** illegal, your English, better than before, **but here come hippies with their friendly reefers** of postcommunist bosses with old **and summer towers instantly too high.** style flavors, your subway's marble and rats, **There'll be another time to tell you why.** hypnotic life in the eyes of police patrols, **For now let's talk of nonsense, trivial chatter,** the regular and the special force. Let's **and laugh at every pun, at every joke,** find some wheels and go us, you and I, to one **without pretending to know literature** of those bars on the river at Taganka, based **or philosophy for that matter.** on an ex cruise boat, no music in one of the rooms. If we did not need to talk we wouldn't be Russian. May memoirs flutter in the glint of darkening windows, while mattresses all fall silent in the district, or sleep descend, or may sleep descend (and kill our holy history for a while) so we may breathe again.

Hymn

The self, that murky pond full of perceptual small fry, scum, water-weeds, over whose surface tension glides the water-fly of a conscience. The lips sip coffee, seem agglutinative, the tongue lapping, blabbing. Stingingly, **The courtyard's bamboo looks with many eyes** your spoon hallucinates **over you with your book and easy-chair.** bleak roses. Self-knowing matter, **The lamps hang on—in every light-bulb cries** the Cicada Muse sobs: nib **your clear obstruction of my life's despair.** me with pain, articulate me with **A line of Gogol flees into the grass** beats of blood, measurements of breath. **with the agility of a grasshopper.** I'm so Lizbethan. The conscience hisses, **Our tea stands cold. A deeper blue and softer** bites with tragic energy, but **turn the inflections of your summer dress,** misses. Night air engages and **darker your long red hair. A quick mirage** Apollo bids me to make music, **of recollection nods over your page** dies a violet in a crucible, lingering **its full agreement like a transparent orchid,** finger. (Suffice it to say, as we **but over my page glows a haze. "Enough"—** Sufis say. Hymn to Apollo, **whispers the spine, hungry thoughts leap with life,** eh gymnosperms turn to **and your sweet belly is big with our child.** flowers! Dionysus drink my eyes! Nymphalids are a kind of butterflies, insect nymphs, as the / sky spreads its stellar solitaire / from over here to over there. Something in anything resists becoming something else, while . . . Tsss, perhaps I should here close the list.

Moi aussi j'aime les nuages qui passent là-bas

You can tell by the lips of modern sensibility the α, the λ and smoky rockies of, the peripeteia and other accouterments of our civilization, or civ. Zesty, zesty, as will bear repetition, way *Those cirrus wisps swept off from stratus floors,* zesty, as will *those ineluctable revolving doors* bear more repetition, zesty *into something painfully blue and radiant,* beats zesty beats *something painfully blue and disobedient,* zesty the heart of *those dark propellers shredding the white fog,* contemporaneity, *assaulting the beclouded underdog,* zesty beats as zestfully as *while over those cumulonimbus piers,* pounds. The heart is a *beyond their floating Boards of Overseers,* shuttle cock, dives *through floodgates of the utmost clarity,* through cloud after *of the utmost clarity and sincerity,* cloud of strife all its life on *you can observe the oceanships of state* plumes of laughter. It *sail shipfuls of shoplifters to their fate* thrives, it appreciates *and shuffle sundry prisoners of delusion* battle. So badminton, *to their final solitary seclusion.* badminton for our privileged colleagues, battledore for their cool cellulose spouses, outdoors, towards a suburban architecture where every shim shines, a gem. I am there by choice. My heart craves amore, amore con carne.

Odessa Herring 1983

Odessa is a port city, it's kinda close to the sea. Let's sit down on a bench and relax a few minutes under this old shady chestnut tree. Eh? Fresh paint? Fine, let's sit farther down in the open. Have you brought your reading matter? **It would be nice in an ideal world,** Good, save it for the herring! Drink beer **shedding ordeal, becoming all-entwirled** in this red heat? Are you nuts? Think **in contemplation, rising above haste,** of your heart, to say nothing of the brain. **to know perfectly-tasting strawberries' taste,** Imagine well how you will feel **to see the pencil raise its perfect tip,** when you're 70, not 17. The beach? We **to watch perfectly-flitting swallows clip** can go there later. Chill man. This is **messages out of nirvanescent skies,** 1983 — there is nothing you can do about it. **to wear armors of perfect alibis,** It's nice to see some foreign tourists around. **to strum on a perfected lute, become** They are friendly toward us, interested in **the perfect match for my perfect madam,** Russia. But our generation's so dumb. **to filter life through perfect harmony,** Glad school is over for good, as they **to wed poetry to the economy,** say in English. What did you say? What time is **to tackle mathematics with the One,** it? Fuck how lonely it is fuck how lonely **then honk that perfect swan-song and be gone.** even with people, with friends around, and it continues so without a change. Plus, boy, I don't like this one bit. This book is giving me ideeers. Besides, it's beginning to rain. This pissing rain will drown us, according to my brownies. So, open the escape route. Let's bail.

Seeing

Stubbornly staid, distantly approachable stand statistics, a wind tossed tray flaps by, we have never consumed so much air, we have never driven so much gas, it disgusts me to spot ***The Hague dawns through my yawning every morning.*** the ***They say, Philip, it's 7 a.m., get up!*** ingénue still hidden be-***My head still buzzy with the coffeeshop,*** hind the newspaper, ***I dash for fresh espresso. Not a thing*** unseen to a world of ***stirred in the city while I slept. No gilder*** opinion glass, unstut-***clicked in a cab. No insect sensed a breeze.*** tered by his predi-***It's hard for me, a casual beholder,*** lections, stern literatures ***ever to find more peaceful nights than these.*** descend into the ***The tram will take me, the martini make me.*** the cash bin, heck ***They bring me very far and very near*** to it, I have taken off my ***under the chestnuts of Statenkwartier,*** coat to the to the crowds ***whose conflorescent flambeaux may mistake me*** of trusting, of ***for an inquisitive diplomat for I say*** acquiescing daily into the ***what up to them on every passing day.*** elementary appertain of copper calicoes on a pendulum line, to let be but a tiny shatter of marrow, I again sip the treasure of laps, I'll be getting out of here shortly, but not soon enough not to have seen all I must see.

Stargazing

There was treble trouble upon us when the clouds drifted close to the ground, their stainless keels plowing over our noses standing at human tallth in the labyrinthine staccato of rain with its street-*Fraternal as television, the day reclines* car refrain. A footloose *into twilight. The olive-colored outlines* inclination printed all *of homes gain obscure clarity. The yards* over downtown's soaked *disintegrate, hoist by their own petards.* skull of visual glass, face *Weirdly over our oblate spheroid* of atmospheric behavior, fickle *the slow sky streams its stellar celluloid* Visigoths of skim mist, *until sleep makes the body leave behind* migrating east, captured *the ruminations of its lonely mind.* fresh pastures and fisher ham-*Silent stars under white-hot torture toss,* lets from Salem to Ipswich *but they have nothing curious to confess.* and the offshore islands, *Socrates says, "Say goodnight to the poets.* blinding blinking light-*They believe something and yet they don't know it.* houses with an *All night they gaze like idiots at the stars,* equine wingedness, then *babbling in cosmogonic metaphors."* back and wrapping with full power around the Hancock Tower, and with a lurch around Trinity Church, obliterating swanboats, squishing ye antique bagel shoppes, wet pub-crawling in heaps of screwy lilacs and other old timer flora.

Discipline

Evening bells have chimed for vespers over at St. John's, and the sun has set and let all bygones be bygones. Daylong from my one true love there has not come a word, and I sit **Sometimes a moment of the old razdraz** alone and languish **builds to internally harass my ass** by this ancient board. **along the nerves in harmonies of jazz** Shards of the hardest **(lacking recording equipment, alas).** avantgarde glow in the **I feel tremendous violence within** dark. Though my homing **and want to kick the fucker in the crotch** dove departed full **or perpetrate some other ancient sin** of buoyant cheer, it **(which one it doesn't matter very much).** brought back no **And yet my brain cells hang on in control,** word of answer **spanning the two poles of a great divide,** from the lighthouse **for man is neither avalanche nor storm.** pier. The number's **Absorbing shock is the perfected form.** been disconnected. **You don't let this stuff out, it hits inside.** As the stars come **Our lives contain so many things we hide.** out to fix me in their icy view, poor things, they cannot imagine how much I love you, how I'd laugh and cry with gladness if you only would come along and break my sadness and my solitude.

A Stately Goodbye

Just as money glows at the end of each parasitic statement
so the great chanciness of art never precludes the ghostly
possibility of pay, albeit the arrangements are phallo-
cephalic. As phallocephalic as magic shows on the road
on a tablecloth of the cacti
or in pots on doilies in a dream,
what else would be a good example to take?
Though possible worlds are none of my business
philosophers and poets are parasites
wideeyed hallucinarians of the sublime.
Poverty is a friend we must say goodbye to
temporarily my boat is sailing tomorrow
up the Charles to the bottom of love
but I love means I have to leave
some day tomorrow some day soon.
It's wicked amazing how you
have grown on me how I don't want to leave you
what am I gonna wish you what am I gonna give you
one drop more is galore one more hello
as I pass Emerson as you pass Boylston.
Sir that was nice.

For Stephen Sturgeon

no more seagull cigar lapel
no more apple by apple pluck
more no more more
foxtail of all everything
polychrome programmatic
but the taking on of
with a certain problem of presentation
pure presentation no emotion no rationality
but yes nationality and a certain
television off television off
exactly what the eye dreams

Things happen as if not happening,
you call without really calling,
sounding not exactly yourself.
The night bursts at the seams but stays the same.
Everything convulses placidly
in the limpid glasswork of
automatic callbox encasements,
and now it's me phoning without phoning,
checking in while not checking in.
The ugly (just normal) dial pipes up a tune,
sounds vaguely like the Marseillaise
except it's all on one note.
Wash me across those zoned echoes.
I am ringing from nowhere,
still barely ringing of half believed hollows.
And who will tune us up tomorrow?
Who knows, that's later,
let's make it through this one first.

Hold that Thought

To have been someone who had
nothing but nothing, a shadow wall
in betrayal of its zigzag wasp.
The ocean's finally getting to me here,
creeps up on me in relentlessness
upon relentlessness.
Here is the impossible for you.
From here it is at all
unfeasible to call you,
wishing to remain fully and firmly
incommunicado
for a short li'l while.
Beep-me-later-dot-com.
Best to not say
what and whereat we are,
who at, what at we stare,
nor is it wisest to exhibit
departive temperatures
just as yet, best
to kiss existence as best we can
in the true face.
Hold that thought.
We have eternity long
to absorb the rest.

Unhappening

There's a lacuna in my life as I know it that I don't know.
A strangely-shuffled light spreads over that patch,
solid line turns to dotted. Beyond a stone's flight
the village road cannot be seen in the lilac dusk.
Or is it morning, and you just woke and the hayloft is balmy?
What if it were truly possible to live
our lives backwards, just like that. Suppose everything
were predetermined and indeed swirled in eternal recurrence,
after the Big Bang the Big Crunch replayed it all backwards
and you saw yourself young, calluses smoothing out,
voice changing to a higher pitch,
pubic hair growing back in, disappearing.

Morning

Local cries for local, distant for distant.
Oven of knify long phosphorescent
testimonies, the soul in common parlance,
whenever thus touched blends
the Syracuse of your presence
with the ports of my syzygy.
The morning is magnified in the slots of Saturday mail.
The pussy willow reblossoms,
a link bridge falls open in the mainframe
as morning drones on
flanked with brick cornices lined
with shadowless eucalypti.
Where are we, where in the world are we?
Transient, sun-drunk, we fray the silk,
we ride the nerve.

Facts of Life

Big fiefdoms of leaves,
beehives of griefs,
companies of thieves—

conglomerates of these,
a worldwide disease,
are anywhere you breathe.

If you haven't yet thought
that you are sold and bought,
you haven't thought aught.

The policy is signed,
now it can only bind,
whether or not you mind.

these pages turn cold in the wind
the hand fears to attack them
but the mind's doodles persist
its having been to hell
helps understand the Comedy
maybe but mainly it hangs
on what what there's left to focus on
not much
principally its own outline
against a cracked surface
mighty cracked surface thoroughly cracked surface
yet with whole pieces of the whole
of the unquiet

In this vat of wishful hearts
life still practices its arts
while the brain sublimely hurts
with the thoughts that it asserts.

In this well of vacant stare
the disjoint and joined appear
as to the lamenting ear
words die frozen on the air.

Revolution

But we want poetry that goes de
de de de de de duh
Duhfamilriazung Ah zo
drrr drrr drrr drrr
dramatiqually Duhfamilriazung
Ourself zo
that oui oui oui oui oui
oui can no longer recognize Ourself
cuz oui wanna escape from Ourself
decompftstrumction o' dze lyrrhic szelf
dze smart fart art of the heart
yahahahahayahoo
flabby backwards echo ahoy choy
yahoohaha Yankee google gender
ouch doodle google do-goooooog1e
rev01utionary! (a pass from the ass)
new1y=pa10ted expecrementalism
we send 0urse1f in2 in-volunta3
ex<[le}-pe<riod>-{cre]mentalism!
Libermancipation thru inn ovation!
Innerovation!!!
We're gonna fucken
empower coprophagic interspecies transgender
sexual politiqs in the municipal graveyard tonight
climbing over the fence defile boldly cuz
bodily in the wet earth
#the important is the %political%
thus wanq wanq wanq wanq wanque
paralogiq paralogiq paralogique
in the fresh grave
decommpftsructing mainstream sexuality
vanilla poetics oh no we're taking risks here
\\ puckeroblematizing | 'accepted"
metabolism {hahaheeooha yep/ ^metaBlowism
"————not afraid to take risks————"

necrotic tic necrotic tics
postLiposuction arse and tits
Thus easily af4ded
all spirits re5ed
feeling tight ~ good
self-banished from the shelf
of the lyrrhic szelf
once and for hell

Homage to Paradox

Some moments are not best served by self-explication,
nor by ancient self-justi- or -purification
nor by Romantic self-atonement,
nor by self-anything-at-all. They are Zen
moments, neither "nor" nor "or,"
neither "now" nor "then." They are
moments when paradox-mongering works well.
Thank you, boy and lady, for making paradoxes so available, so
inviting to monger. Let's monger us one right here,
for whatever one cannot speak of one must forever
moan in paradox. It expressly cools to state the obvious
into the oblivious—paradoxingly!—hat I could profusely and insistently
call upon to call and be called
(sail me out of here into a new world
on wings of a bird on wings of a bird)
into a tight Pandora's box of jokes, hoax and paradox.
For it's not like you thought, have or had thought before,
nor like ever you've thought or you'd thought or'd have thought,
nor is it like you would not have not thought of it were you asked,
nor also the kind of creeper structure with which you are acquainted
and of which you are of a high opinion—
the day-to-day creeper structure of everything into which you tap—
no not that kind of framework but rather a thing of kindness,
a thing of nerve, the kind-of-thingness that hides
behind essentially a family of dumb blogs, a grackle of "projects,"
droves of "sequences" and "longer pieces" (Marx, they make me puke)
everybody is "working on a longer piece right now," where dribblo-
neuro-placebo coils in smoke and everything is based
on some *large* number (where nine is already an oucher)
and the the (sic) thick and thin era of posthumodeternity
has already set in prepaid by voucher
(as I trust hear myself to gather
and must cry out in prophesy though I'm no professor).

That's exactly when paradoxicularity marches in handy on hind legs only along with sundry other dribblefernality and dribbleferentiality bottomlessly deployed as the equivalent of PTN (PolyTrimethylene Naphthalate) in poetics. Mang! What's "there"?
The locomotive into station chugs,
but empty is.
Its people are not there.
I left them these graffiti on the bench.

Cicadas

Wife's figured out to turn off cicadas.
She whistles, they shut up. Damn,
how do I turn them back on?

Book Tongue

penal servitude of speech toilings of grammar
and perpendicular toilings of words through their long paradigms
lisped laments of linear elements of syntagmatic elements
the telescopic spying of supersegmental intrusions intonation
stress pleophony dive in rings sememes piping through out
into who knows happenstranscendence and then slim flocks
of deliberate orchestration besitting highwires of logic
hazen penetrative sediments of visual impress
embossed bottles of manuscripts
with cinnabar space dice preambles at times
books truncated to their leaves and reconstituted
miniature illuminations mostly faded but some
still quite bright amid the frozen parcels of speech
the old quill is dead now but the books are alive

My name is Wormswurst, I give back to men their Zen.
I switch their here now with my there then.

Their stories of the past forgotten
Lay many generations protein,

But when our new spores come to life,
We sing them from within a hive.

We show a multitude of claws
and form a multitude of laws.

We see a world in groping mittens.
Will not obey! This music leads me,

This music leads me, leads me where?
Oh how it leads me! I don't care!

Hotel

Time to recount the sparrows of the air.
Seated alone on an elected stair,
I stare as they appear and disappear.

Tonight the deck supports tremendous quiet,
although the twilight is itself a riot.
I'm glad I'm staying here, not at the Hyatt.

My pen, eye, notes, watch, whiskey glass and hell
all hang together comfortably well.
Pain is my favorite resort hotel.

Sharks

Those Black Sea sharks are only half-shark sharks
or maybe one-third or one-fourth-shark sharks,
sometimes they even seem like baby sharks,
diminutive in stature, harmless to humans.
Nah, if you want to be a real big shark,
perhaps you've got to be a White Shark shark.
Then maybe you'll get even photographed
on the sand, harpoon unseen,
a dozen happy children on your back.

Life

After a bad night's sleep, while still undressed,
depressed and rested, rested and depressed,
instead of going crazy or berserk,
I smile to brush my teeth, prepare for work.

The Next Level

To advance to the next level of enlightenment,
say those ancients,
you must first teach another,
for teaching requires perfected knowledge.
I don't know how it is in matters spiritual,
but in life mundane
teachership gets away with plenty.
My father taught me English before he knew it himself:
he read to me from *Phoenist the Bright Falcon*,
Russian folktales in English translation,
explaining the English sentence by sentence
in his own fashion. Plus he had a shortwave VEF radio,
so the World Service of the BBC
(" ... first the news, read by Brian Empringham ... ")
reigned supreme in the house, interspersed with brainwashing
from the Radio Moscow World Service.
I first learned the differences between the two worlds
by marking disparities of grammar and intonation.
On the other hand I don't know how to ride a bike,
because somehow I've never had one.
My daughter, at six, cycles swiftly on her two-wheeler.
She learned to bike just a couple of weeks ago.
I gripped the handlebars to help her find her balance,
and in telling her that pedaling is like walking,
that air holds you up like water,
I concealed from her my ignorance, but not for long.
The next thing I knew was, she braked expertly,
turned back to me sharply and declared:
"Now it's *your* turn!"

I wish to live my life like a house insect
in an insecticide free environment
wend my way out of the world into a corner
wherewith I can identify fully
and just sit there and think long thoughts
once in a while to crawl under the curtain
to see snow falling
across my emerald compounded eye
not understanding
and buzz off without pain
impossible

Global bacteria local euphoria
Chinese wisteria US hysteria
Euro magnolia
Caucasian acacia
whose helicopter
knows just what it's after

Trudged afternoons
drenched anniversaries
French macaroons
Sunday adversities
at universities
helium balloons

Frowned baking stuff
militant energy
aren't you enough
for a terse threnody
a dirge's stuff
with sharps much rough

Whisper in gloom
this far through solitude
sweep the left magnitude
with a dust broom
in the mind's room
adjust your attitude

Folklore

Bruno went across the water
saw a crab upon a slab
stuck his hand into the river
and was ouch grabbed by the crab.

Urbane Suburbia

Magic coals and olives @ our rambunctious BBQs, with always some suburban author ragging on Simon & Schuster or HMCO over rosebush and shrimp, and you just stand there nodding. I **We like to sketch things in our best intended,** sometimes meet **light-carving vision, fishing with the story line.** up in the great **As a laborer, it becomes relatively hard to revolve** upstairs an **when you grow tired down, eleven to twelve.** aspiring politico. **Music casts for extra relaxation; I give in,** Our attic JFKs are **the way which chimes my glories. The heart,** nightingales even **a thief in oneself, raps sans a cooing problem.** more than the **You dig the situation and sympathize. Tangled,** poets, singing **the Persian lamb of a constructive boat** to us as they do of their **ruffles the night prunes.** administrivia. Zima is puke swill, no **I segment myself into parts** thanks. White Overproof Rum's my **and go about visiting friends.** poison. I wanna pee on the grass, **Celebrant, celebrant is my dowry,** horticulturally parlaying. **for I'm being wed to poetry!** Jonquils are pralines. Should I also go roofing? They got caviar up there, chance of a better education. How you have captured my gut, lady emerald rock rhododendron. Short-lived thaw in the German Democratic Republic of the mind.

A Quarry of Words

My city is very small, but I own it. Battalions of brazen brass could not destroy it if it saved their ass. Ministering to their wounds, they must be joking, militaristically speaking, but I simply open my umbrella and the ***Obscure as rage, the willow clings to clay,*** wind blows them away, from ***an avalanche of twigs in sharp display.*** here to Hollywood & to, via the ***The mast is wedded to the mist, the mist*** movies and the movie trailers, ***hangs on modalities of may and must.*** Uttar Pradesh. Monkeys galore ***Mute and astonishing, the crested moon*** catapulting from banyan trees ***swings brimming on the strings of Humayun*** shoo them away and bite ***and rattles like a keg of flotsam honey*** off their determination. ("Shooed ***delivered on a tong of surplus money.*** by Monkey Folk.") Delicatessenly ***I, co-enslaved and collared by the bay,*** Firdousian, the elevator, it clicks, ***forever groan and grope at what to say,*** disadmitting us into a pushcart ***diving through rocks to palpable solutions.*** lounge, filled with chilled tea ***Only the quarry wants my revolutions.*** urchins, comfits on yodel platters, ***Dry ether fills the hollows of the earth.*** a skelter-helter caboodling down ***Creative life, acute mineral dearth.*** riverside stalks, so. I happen to have tomorrow. After all those discomfortable positions (in threads)—freedom! Stay alert and wish you were always here, with meaning. With no meaning, why would we wish to stay? Ahoy, life opens a new book to an old page!

19 March 2004
For Igor Tkachenko

I paint my keyboard in the wildest colors
The notes they have lain fallow for too long
To strum a song to strum a song to strum a song
The poet sang the point is not in dollars

In the tectonic murmurs of the gong
Of D and in the concave mirror purls
Of A, who feeds these quasi-stellar
Vibrations of a mortal waltz

Who leads them and especially where
Away into what lurid stratosphere
Sarcastically governed by F#

Amen It's time perhaps to shut my harp
And sleep on silver syllables and rave
Until the sun spins out to pave the wave

Crocodile

In this modern age and style
everything is crocodile:
crocodile purses, crocodile tears,
crocodile sized chandeliers.

Purse me something crocodile,
weep me something crocodile,
light that candle and redial
something likewise crocodile.

A clueless guppy by the shore
I'd rather swim forevermore,
yet I must ponder for a while
ways in which I'm a crocodile.

Beautiful, innocent and vile,
King of the Ganges, of the Nile.

Farewell

Let us stare now into this
Metaphysical abyss
And with certainty and grace
Trace our insights into space

No let's not stare let's go home
Each to his cold private tea
From now on you're on our own
Farewell to philosophy

A Midsummer Night's Stroll

I.

I am a man. I've lived alone. I've been in love. I've played with fire, cursed the telephone, and basked in verse, in verve, and also *Humid, terrestrial, mixed, nongenderspecific,* **have occasionally** *day's tumult ushers in an evening with a lone* **moved a woman's** *shut icecream stand, false promises of cone* **heart, although I also,** *and scoop near Central Park. Juneific* **famously, had such an awk-** *are the silhouettes of people dreaming by,* **ward start. Amazed at** *lips, lit cigarette tips, thoughts and tulips streaming by* **how much** *along dimly hospitable park lamps toward eleven* **symmetry a life** *with an occasional rev of internal combustion* **can still support, I** *wafted across from nearabouts.* **stare in rapt near-idiocy, like a** *"What's this you are talking about, Sarah?"* **foreign passport, and** *you hear a voice, and the reply, "I'm sorry,* **April's Persian lilacs** *but what was I supposed to do?" Two bats* **all bloom straight into** *dash through a silver stretch of atmosphere.* **my face, and various** *What she was supposed to do we never hear.* **other blossom, too, depending on each case, while you are softly tangible, while you are sweetly mine. We're existentially wise, we're mortally divine.**

II.

All whispers know where whispers go and lusters where with lusters flow, and when your palm is in my palm, just as my poem is in your poem, look at this stellar, cellular, organic life of mine, the general and particular, the gross (as well as fine) intentions I epitomize. Look, seeing through its thin disguise the bleary sky whose weepy eyes have rained us a surprise. A lightning bolt's protruding hand snatched past us, far and brief, and as I hold you in my arms, you fill me with belief. Don't wonder if and how, much stranger than right now, the hyacinth of sorrow may blossom forth tomorrow.

There is a sparkling tone to how you speak, a quickness to your whisper, an implied correctness in your ironies. We stride along emphatic benches in the weak light bristling eloquent dark. Pine, elm and oak fall silent now to hear you tell a joke— something about a man and a mandrake; I think it cute and laugh like Captain Drake. We then explore the vagaries of light found underfoot by lamps, and kiss. "Beatrix, will you still need me when I'm thirty-six?" You favorably mumble that you might, and throw a willing arm around my nape. I reassure you that there's no escape.

III.

The stars in liquid decadence reclaim their lost positions, all knotty dispositions dissolved in limpid dance. They offer us their stardom. Oh, we could sympathize with them, but instead, we set eyes with them upon that higher tsardom, that real of love and reason. Our lengthy cigarettes crackle with dry regrets during the rainy season, but we ignore their humors, their melancholy murmurs, decline ascetic rigors, welcome straight facts, clear figures, where laws concerning numbers come plumed with midnight sounds, and spirits stir from slumbers like angels out of clouds.

Another couple floats up through thickened ink
into the field of vision, to redissolve
leaving a thin trail of perfume and love
and visual recollection in the pink.
Cicadas cataract from tree to tree.
A mock nightingale trills, then two, then three.
We cut short across grass and leaves (then four),
encountering no one on our slight detour
where, negligibly burdened with a sixpack,
a master and his bulldog rustle on,
a small red light fixed to her furry back.
We are too busy with our love to see them.
Tomorrow we'll be going back to Boston.
Three cheers for Central Park at height of season.

A Ghazal
For John Kinsella

Today we turn to times more remote: I offer to your attention a ghazal by emperor Bahadur Shah II, also known to Urdu poetry lovers under the *nom de plume* of Zafar (1775-1862). Zafar lived a colorful life to a **language action heft me fatum dei** tragic end. An aesthete rather than **eagerly recast upon the seaboard** a genuine leader, a "philosopher prince" **there will be no water corroboree** constantly dependent on the English **there will be but spindrift of the word** rulers of India, he was destined to **there will be no civvy street engagements** become the very last Moghul **only life in syntax on the lam** emperor in history. He was 82 when the **moreover no game plan in the lab** great Indian Mutiny of 1857 broke out. **only lignum and pigment arrangements** Fearing for his life, he accepted **behind glass and over the glass walls** the nominal leadership of the revolt **adjectival thor in the dishwasher** and was subsequently dethroned by the **lime on letterhead who can be sure** English when the revolt was put down. **of the pithy pepper of these calls** He was exiled to Burma, where he died **language cut with language scoops and drains** some four years later. We **surfs of hopes against a reef of pains** should resist the temptation to see Zafar's generally broken-hearted, disillusioned poetry as informed by this tragic reversal of fate. The pessimisms of his verse are rhetorical: he wrote all his verse before the final calamity of his life, then nothing thereafter.

Commencement Walk

Landiens and gentelmurfs, some phoenix here ha' bin tryin' to sow seditioun among yom folks. Tha's why we're here, to talk about it. That gross misdeed, I tell ya, my young ladies and fellers, is mighty skanky to my mind, if you'll ***As abstract as an afterlife, the skyline*** pardon the proletarian exposition. This ***suddenly dives, followed by weary eyes.*** is some tough shit to be reportin'. How ***Two cyclists pedal down the red-brick lane.*** much have you known of there to ***The sun-struck collegiate pavement dries.*** be an ingenuity that would cause ***With waves of Baltic ivy overflowing*** a blooper like this into happenin'? Who, ***and winked at by occasional stained glass,*** I ask you, is gonna assume respon- ***wrought-iron grilles accompany our going*** sa-bility? The snifter blinks and ***past rhododendrons in our slow progress.*** boggles! 'Atta gwerk ideer! N other ***No fresh nor uppermiddleclassman can*** words, givin' you just the meat and ***explain away the necessary pattern*** moral of the whole story, permit me to tell ***exemplified. Wake up, walk on, resist*** y'uns real short. Underderstanderably, ***saying you know what causes you to walk,*** we got mighty persnickety at the ***to stalk your prey, or to be prey and stalked.*** stinkin' beast, the wood pussy out ***We are not free. Life leads us by the wrist.*** there. And I'm tellin' you like Mr. Judge, I conduct me *own* investigation. I dinna hafta find the guy "guilty," nor "unguilty." All I cared wuz mother justice (to our errin' souls) hadtabe served! He had ta be brought down so we flattened him ta road pizza good and simple.

I Am not Used to Using a Cell Phone

Thoughts of tableware and under the table ware. Hiccupping eucalypti bask in the moderate sun. The artist's palate seeks out the rarest of the rare, the raw. Hurry, there are upper end pescoovolactovegetarian restaurants here, Her mind, abruptly bent on running out ***très bourgeois but for a change we're*** slamming the house door in that freebee play ***"celebrating in style." Hi there,*** glared back in anger. Her gray Chevrolet ***the City and countryside! And may*** out of the private driveway past fresh doubt ***May melancholy humors waft away,*** and paint. Few driving men remarked her slight ***may magic shit of birds forever*** figure in rear view mirrors. On red she knew ***by the squashed grapeful pour down*** she'd stop and weep and drive on. Raindropped light ***to cure the soil's pedestrian*** glassed in the length of Commonwealth Avenue. ***indigestions, to promote both*** The dim lit constellations that had drowned ***watermelons and waterlilies, may*** her windscreen's blank careening intellect ***intimate friendships brew on each*** resolved no puzzle in their sudden zoom ***cicada-ridden campus, grammatical*** where through a runny sky she saw unwind ***ganja sprout throughout the drug*** garlands of hopelessness and ill effect ***free zone in shoots of gigantic graffiti,*** marqueeed over the night's aquarium. ***some of them "way" witty. Hiya, the City! Missing our exit, we hurry hurtling back. The dang cell rasps its B flat. We're hungry. And though we're breaking some appointments here, let crabmeat bloom and the skies be high. Something like that!*** as they say in California.

Poetry Month Poem

Come, poet, shed your trite sentimentations and turn on your kenny, tragic mercantilism. Unto everything its cost! Be tough, act rational in a society that persecutes its poet ***Everything waits for its appropriate hour.*** w/ indifference. ***The flask that chokes its wine to vinegar*** Every creature, ***can turn vinegar back to wine again.*** even Ivan the poet, ***There'll be a train and there will be no train.*** will fight for ***A cosmic aesthete with high tragic powers*** its survival. If ***alone again among machines and flowers*** they still refuse ***marks constellations of high abstract things.*** to give you $$, ***His tall contemplative meanderings,*** raise hell, threaten to ***where every lemma blooms toward the good,*** withhold your ***progressively advance him through the wood*** poetry. Tell ***of false appearance. Quit the elevator*** them without ado that ***and further proceed by the escalator*** strictly they gotta, socie- ***down, toward the taxi waiting by the exit.*** ty, with its forked ***Hop in, hoping to God you can afford it.*** butt, with its cloven brain, wet hoof, pay for their sheer existence, which comes from poetry. It's poetry doesn't give a pong about society; it's society depends on poetry for not becoming soulless morons.

Rhetoric

To say, neigh or bray something meaningful
is already an act of
auctioning oneself off in units
of communication, an exercise in
while silver seagulls
cascaded through the wintry sky
as if swooping down
their practiced wings sharp against the wind
then alongside a neon tableau they suddenly
salt and peppered into view . . .—
or an exercise for example along the
tentative/elective lines of *we propose*
to log system wide error messages
and have the system call <u>the administrator (Admin)</u>
by default & offer ability to unlog error messages
wholesale via an intuitive single click option
*from the administrator's screen—*or even
a workout like *mental mice munch*
at memorable moments of my life
and I too am a sort of ex-mouse
genetically reengineered into a horse.
Hoist high the horseshoe. That's my motto.
Hit down hard with the hoof.
Say neiiiiiiiiggghhh!!!!!!!
Yeeeea; equine eloquence is what the exercise is in.
Romping cattycorner at cross-clouds-of-grass lacrosse,
out he comes, that winged horse,
over flat skies of the soil,
all a-kick with elation, wanting
and *yeeeees; indeeeed;* fully intending
to say or bray something meaningful.

Target Practice
For Eugene Gorokhovsky

The telephones are cast into oblivion. The night's caprice, a long slim flower-treading murky cat is with us in the garden and can see the Milky Way's overhanging udder all along our dirt road. ***The only touch of autumn to our car*** Our eyes swim brilliantly ***(which only xists nsome transcendental realm*** in our galaxy. We, ***which actually nevers gone so far*** with a silent pipe in a tin lizzy ***as tactually xist, as toverwhelm*** parked on the hill, lights off, the ***us with itstark reality) perceives*** radio off, in the silence of Maine. ***its own autumnal self as vertigo.*** The fireflies wind their woe amid ***Ours troubled tissue knows not where to go.*** dew, twinkling with ***The silly yellow reach of willow leaves.*** the faulty periodicity of ***Tho I am foreigner, I ling this lang*** July. The evanescent sky ***sufficient to impress the bearded drove*** takes on an anthracite hue. ***of native speaker, of pedantic locust,*** Barn swallows in their swift ***for I am god of language, I shall hang*** sleep under the black eaves ***my verbal portrait in their sacred grove*** dream properties of space ***and shoot at it at leisure, when I'm focused.*** among the ancient apple trees. A lightning bolt falls, the stars shut off. Another sinks to the hilt into some buttock of earth. Storm. Unlike a coyote, we wait it out in the car, under the black wet sieve of leaves. Then we return.

The Cure

Backchat backed, back out. Backset bagged, baked. Basked basket, beached. Beget begged, bequeath, beset biased bigot, big shot, booked & boozed bouquet boxed, bucked bucket, busied, buzzed-faced facet. Fagged, faked faucet, fished. *They say our sense of the absurd in life* Fixed, fogged, fused, fussed & paced. *stems from a backward step we all perform,* Packed packet, passed. { Pass out *in our hesitant minds from time to time,* peached! } Peaked, peak out! Pecked, *permitting thus ourselves to see ourself* peg out picked. Picket. Pick out piked, *from an objective distance. Finding no* pissed pocket ($). Poised, poked, posed, *justification, reason butts a wall.* posit. Pouched, puked, pushed. Viscid, vised *The mathematics that describe our fall* visit. Voiced, vouched. Carbon, carbon *from stable meaning through a vertigo* 12, carbon 13, carbon 14, carven Cervin, *of the absurd are eminently clear,* chaffiest, cheapest, chiefest, chippiest, Chop- *becoming clearer still by drawing nearer.* piest, chubbiest, chuffiest, cobbiest *Self-scrutiny with its magnifying glass* copyist! Corban, Cuban cubist. Cuppiest, *indicts each segment of the soul at issue.* gabbiest gabfest: gappiest, goofiest ... *But sense is simply sex, and when I kiss you,* safest! Sappiest, scabbiest, seepiest! *hot hallelujahs smother each alas!* Shabbiest scarfpin scorpion. Serbian, sharpen shearpin! Soapiest sophist, soppiest, soupiest, suavest, sweepiest, zippiest bigtoe. Busty facti, Fausta? Feisty feste, Fichte! Fie, fiesta! Fusty Pashto pasta paste, pasty pesto, pesty pigsty, piste Pistoia, poste Pushtu. Vasty vesta, vestee vista, Maestro!

The Seeded Friend of Humankind Is Cashed

Standard and Poor's (S&P) is a world leader in financial information and analytical services. It provides the financial and business community with analytical tools, accurate and time-sensitive information, and expert com- *The seeded friend of humankind is cashed,* mentary that facilitate and in- *but I have found a place where more is stashed,* fluence decision-making *a lab where every leaf is dried to that* about investments. S&P's CUSIP/ *word-perfect flam and readiness to act* ISIDPlus CD-ROM product, deve- *on every syllable. The moot trapeze* loped by Kanda Software in 1997, *of sense remotely utters thank you, please* provides an interactive environ- *and marches down directly to the page* ment for quickly locating security *to perpetuate its sensuous brigandage.* identifiers and descriptions for half *Semantic hemlocks melt to tilted tiles,* a million CUSIP and ISID issuers *and titles brim with paratactic styles,* and millions of Corporate, Municipal, *and elfin horses of the golden ring,* Government, Mortgage Backed and *who come to spell a wish on everything,* Private Placement issues, and is- *gallop with lust and neighing through the bong,* sues from the Internation- *god-naughty and immensely drawn to song.* al Securities Identification Directory. The product is fitted with a powerful search and retrieval system designed to find information on issuers based on complex search criteria, with ability to print or export search results to another Windows application.

The Nut Club

The Nut Club is the most ancient club in the world. Some assert that one of the founders of the Nut Club was none other than Prometheus, who brought ("took," or stole) fire from the gods for the use of humanauts (human nuts). *A lithe graffito god, crest upon crux,* History is replete with heroic examples *is trembling on its perch and now will dive* and actions of equally unequalled *on crumbling wall wings through thin rainfall live* heroism. It is all ashine *out of blind passion undersigned by crooks.* with (=full of) heroic examples *This slow power-demarcated August looks* and acts of unequally equaled *with mild contempt, keen-clawed intentions thrive* Nuttishness. Nuts are the *on pallid wanderers from far more deluxe* Au of history! As heaven-gazers, *accommodations in a different hive.* sea-explorers, daydreamers and artists, *Along Encumbrance Lane into the wan* members of the Nut Club have made *familiar Shit Luck Square, whatever they* many contributions to the Great *refer to it here as. This ledge-of-Mars-* Common Basket of Nuts (GCBN). *like tract of town (there I cannot be wrong)* Albert Einstein nuttified physics *continues down three miles in motley gray,* with his epoch-unmaking theories *until we drive back out under the stars.* of relativity. He was one of the most absent-minded men in the world. Once on his way to an important scientific meeting, Einstein telephoned his wife and asked, "Where am I and where am I meant to be?" Mysteriously enough, history is silent as to what she replied.

Zeno's Stoop

I wish the editors had kept the victory scenes but cut out some of the celebrations in this fatal film, I wish the acting behind the acts were shinier at times. Duplicitous and energizing clout of rain. Nature. Don't be timid. Attack if you must with your **A labor fine but hardly lucrative** eyes people who try to trip you, most particularly **must needs remain publicly secretive,** yourself, window-reflected in black. Rained **which passersby will find profoundly strange** weather, whosoever the progenitor, **as I emerge into their visual range** whichever the means of generation, method of **with a blank page, forgetful of the watch.** gratification. The world's cosmetic: the **What is that fellow up to on the porch?** rain's descending escalation—though even **Zeno instructed pupils on his stoop,** our percepts of weather are not without certain **made solid Stoics out of their whole group,** aggression, firm ranks of gray greatcoat **but why does that one loiter in his chair,** clouds seen in terms of "marching against" **as if there were none better anywhere?** the sky, "closing in" on the moon "shield," **Well, he's engaged in an archaic ritual,** "overpowering" (whether or not legitimate**more physical than, say, spiritual,** ly) attempts at luminosity (so it all "darkens") **fashions his lips into a pair of sours** whilst that timid sleeveless "fantastic weather" **and stares at nothing for a couple of hours.**—"the" "other" "weather"—stands in still scare quotes, never by itself. Fog like a boat ride rises in the eye of the beholder. You know what, I really wish the editors had cut the victory scenes as well, but left in the bare bones, etched aquiline scowls, the face shuffle non-stop in the timetable.

Offer

Kindly pick up the party favors! The party needs many favors today,
at this our semiofficial reception. Doesn't matter which party. I'm
proud to have you in the Kremlin, esteemed military guests from far
My mind is a garage without a car. away! Yes, waste no time, start
I whisper my old mantra: check no mar. socializing. And say what,
Albeit my brew is preferably Czech, didjer, didjer read that novel
my current worth has missed the monthly check. where the good
What good did you me, ancient mantra old? spy is captured by an
I have been bold but I got none in gold, operative of the enemy's
vended for beans, a-howling at the moon, secret service, cause they
although it's plain and shining afternoon. primed his alienated ex-
On such a day I can sometimes seem very girlfriend's current boy-
self-interested and even mercenary. friend to establish his location,
Forget Czech brew, Cambridgeport Liquors port. trick him? So our
I have a wife and daughter to support. good guy says: "I am worth
Got none in copper though I have been brave. much less than you
Hey, would anyone care to buy a slave? are offering me. I cost 2 or
maybe 2.5 mln tops, which is way below what you're offering me.
It's out of my league! Even so, with all the money in the world you
couldn't bribe me, motherfuckers, into betraying my government."

Ideers

Bash'um hard with a hunk o' lard, cowboy,
when they come 'ere to seduce our sons and daughters,
the *only* sons and daughters we *have*,
with their damn ideers. They think ideers
are worth somethin' like a Bushel O'Pork
per each. Trahahahaha. They eschew
the feelin's of patriotism, peals of chivalry
'n' private property like. So what does we care
to preserve them as a subspecies? Bein' ourselves
of solid as rock good local stock
'n' rooted in these very hills that we cultivate,
bein' so local that the mind races over
aeons of banjo-tinklin' memory of roots
like echoes in the prairied valley, being
precisely that kinda stock, honest blue grass treadin',
we're buyin' *none* of that Uruguay political correctness.
None, I be tellin' ya m's'ladies!
We automatic'ly
put that subspecies under suspicion, zitwere.
The shmuck (pardon me, Sir, me
umbilical vernacular) hadta be tryin' to
spray us around wi' hi' *curlture*.
He said he be a-dribblin' *learnin'* into our heads
wi' like *critical thinkin'* routines.
But without shittn' y'uns, I muss hereinafter d'claire
his reasonin' ta be sorely wrong an' fallaiches.
In fact, it is beyond fallaiches. Whatever.
Y'uns havin' troubles hearin' or somethin'? We been
on this land for gwerk knows how many a century,
from eras immemorable, and we know,
havin' built these here barns and infrastructure,
we know without prejudice
and in good shape 'n' hope 'n' faith 'n' all
of mind and body like, we know
exact what the heck it cost to keep

the streets of our polity clean,
Partridge and Dingleberry Rock Village Plaza,
positively speakin' straight narrow *clean*.
I do repeat, straight narrow *clean*,
of all yum culturevultures with all yum
cloggin' dog's doo an' piece o'shit ideers.

A Letter to the Antipodes

Vessels of vacuum cleaving to the margin, sailing ever and over into the vacuum clear. Vision's butterfly pinned head down within *I have just met the Holy Cow,* a dewdrop. *That's why I have a Tall Eyebrow*—Where *But she has no Eyebrow at all,* do we come *Whether Diminutive or Tall.* from and who, what are we stuck being? Hard to help to be *In fact, She quite has Neither.* me. In bed-*Tschhht, no One is the Wiser.* wet solitude *You never Know what is on* early experience *This Beyond Reason Season.* lies embedded in memory. Watch out, or they might suspect you with your heels on the ceiling, with your pants over your head, in the mellow antipodes.

Pensées

I wish to be forever déclassé, whether
singing to empties or deciding matters
of substance and authority. Tonight
I let the philosopher out of the bottle
tremulously to walk across the cobweb
of (thoughts and into the omnibus and
bosom of) the understanding.

Snow is a cad. The phlox-plucking
snow. Rude lips whisper
more than the mind knows,
yet it is by whispering
that the mind learns to know
how to whisper
and the body how to understand.

Under a winecolored welkin
and helicopter, tables are people,
snow is a cad.
By citing lacunae and revelations, automobiles
react differently to the spanking new snow.
Some go grumbling,
others just sit where they belong
without moving.

And you, who lead me into
temptation, you all you
amid the crooning environment
brittle monkeys,
brittle little monkeys
who drag me through the custard,
box my ears, choke me and scratch me
and sneeze me in the eye and smile;

who declare me officially insane, a sociopath,
who slip me a $20 bill,
make me insult the security,
make me fall on my bum and elbow and over
my own incisive analysis of Johnny Walker's
black lapel; you who legalize me without
legitimizing very method of sustenance,
you who drench me with cowardice and affection;

who hit me in the floating ribs area,
who jeer and thwack me across the face,
who lead me out of the stable
and transfer me on first demand
to the authorities, all you monkeys,
all you yogurt-hiding,
all you law-abiding,
all you slimy nasty revolting monkeys

and lizards, flies, lowlifes and riffraff!
What in parallel reality do you exactly
want with me, you crucibles?
Do you internalizing think I give a rotary saw
for your opinion? Who do you
meandering, deliberating imagine me to be?
Whom are your mandibles in reference to?
Go identify yourselves. Go budding identify yourselves.
Leave me the remote control alone.
Go take your smoking boots off my chest!
I don't give a barking trapeze or intention
for your norms of intellect,
you rioting grazing periwinkles you!

Ithinkistillcanhear

IthinkIstillcanhear
thepingingofthebells
ifwedontlikeithere
wegoasomewhereelse
distinctlyIremember
themurmursoftherose
ifshedontlikeithere
sheupandelsewheregoes
dailyaswellasnightly
passionsinsinuate
thatiftheyalldontlikeit
theywilllevitate
butImaluckyfellow
myfortunesaregalore
fortheyalllikedithere
andstayedforevermore
sodarlingdarlinganddarling
letsdrinkthislatesttoast
toeverythingthatbeforefalling
temporarilygrows
foreverythingthatsmortal
parksbehindonemotel
underwaytothenext
inandoutofatext

Ideas

doyouthinkImdrawingnear
likethehoovesthatyoucanhear
noImtakinganidea
outofanidea

andImputtinginanother
anotheridea
callthefirstideamother
andtheseconddaughter

looknowintotheidea
ofaprivatelanguage
questioniswhoputitthere
howdiditemerge

wesurelycannottell
butthenwhatthehell
embeddedinthebrain
pardoncomeagain

A taste that loves the classical cliché
and rational construction in the form,
a taste that validates the quick touché
and radical disruption of the norm

both fit into a leather attaché
and consequently will survive the storm.

Benares USA

Imagine winding up hanging out with a bunch of scruffy
old-timer US hippies who believe that hash straightens out
reality, along with an intense contemplation of the stars. They're all
natural bohemians, entirely romantic. They all majored
in geography in college in the 60s. Ashok and I found them by
the Ganges, cool uncles from the Krishna Lodge. They foam
with off-the-cuff poetry, all about their admiration for stars,
among other things, though they still hate betel nuts after all
these years. They have all met Allen Ginsberg, and have all
seen Maharishi Mahesh Yogi on their travels, and touched his feet
in adoration, at one time or another. Sharing an autorickshaw
ride home with one of the Yanks after the party, I ask why he
wouldn't care to return to the US. You see, quoth he, one
American at home is OK, but two Americans equal mass hysteria.

In a Hospital

Don't ask. I can't explain. Roses stream forth deciduous
froth. Smoke exacts its toll, celibacy or not.
Lucid, we grow to grief, faltering past invidious
symmetries still unwooed, battles as yet unfought.
Caves rave. The rivers drone. Flames undertake their functions.
Lives wafting through their silks forget the sky, ablaze
with sanitary vows on peace-inviting unctions.
Unreconstructed revs the context of their maze.
Humanity is near, high, clear. The heart abstracts from
the weft and woof and weed of hours their stellar wood.
One always finds a plot's unmotivated platform.
The owner of this sword is worth its donor's blood.
Across the gates and ghats of the long god-filled plateau
the clouds cast twilight nets into the rivers' breath.
All syllables will swell to one eternal motto.
The mantra spins its lucent path through life and death
and life. All poems conflict. Their lungs are filled with pollen.
Flames argue. Karma takes sheer moments to unfurl.
These dynasties are rain. These dynasties have fallen.
Gods towering through the skies deny the human role,
laugh. Children play with mud. Another rug is needed;
pale conchs are blown; it's time to trade in work for rest.
Innocence comes with peace. Fresh incense is ignited;
and house roofs moan but give no sign that they're distressed.
In prayer and wandering years turn to sand, grow lighter
and lighter. Wet white gauze rises to thirsting lips.
The weather sweats its wrath. Eyes roam through ether, whiter.
Wild goats in essence stride over the sharpest cliffs,
lush brambles bend their heft where bees betray a pattern,
boats sail on sleep. Thoughts drink. Dreams thicken into cotton,
but late-arriving dusk's tinsel is thin and torn.
Quit reading. It'll be dark before you'd count to ten.
The missionary wards, where patient-worship dwells,
are silent, but behind the ashram's wall a river
of life again contracts its tiny private hells,

its true atomic facts, cells of oblivion, liver
of hope. Not even the banks are constant, but the orchards
are foam and mist. They roll and scatter and flake away.
Out on the lakes, in zero wind, the reeds
stand empty, free, awake. With nothing to convey,
they simply stare and are. Why couldn't also we
contain our susurrus and love, why could we not
in some monastic sense as simply stare and be
reed-hearted and attached in root, but not in thought?

Nothing Changes

Furthermore, I will be helpful determining (1) "Stakes in the Ground" —general approaches and specific technologies best suited to the project. I believe that unless the RFP refers to at least a minimal set of high-level approaches (e.g. the use of XML or WebServices, preferred data integration strategies, etc.), the prospective vendors are likely to respond with incompatible proposals, making their objective evaluation difficult. (2) Revenue Models—e-Commerce features that generate no nonsense revenue. Over the years I have mastered the art of effectively mixing and matching various revenue generation methods best suited to the nature of a specific enterprise, in order to maximize my clients' returns on investments. (3) The Optimal Solution—i.e. a solution optimized with an eye to the client's specific needs by streamlining and cost reengineering, including modularizing CM and authoring improvements.

Seeming well natural on its buttered course,
the centipede of treason's on its way.
I walked beyond the terminals today
to wipe its traces on a cloud of gorse.
Hey, holler, man! The year 2000 draws
up its fata morgana epopee
as blooming navels gather on the Bay
like serotonin boosters, but of course
the stars of suds in mystagogue alerts
are always there. The mantelpiece in lush
precaution spins out synaesthetic hurts.
Ozones dry worded on the power brush.
Logs ship and fly, the toasty parakeet
cries nothing ever changes in this heat.

Philosophy & Rhetoric
For Joe Green

With waves of Baltic ivy over-woven, there towers ancient brick. The King of Rhetoric rises to the throne. Ye Boylston professors, bow yer heads in bows, as in woe ye knit yer elocutionary brows. **Where once thick and punitive red dust** Coffee evaporates quick in **imbued with penalties the color red** monstrous doses. The spoon **in marrow's meditation, unsurpassed,** hallucinates airy mimosas. **there glows through lukewarm vertebrae the vita,** The spoon drops **addicting souls to lines. But now in dread,** to the floor, the moon **well-manned monstrosities address the issues too** saucer cracks, as **and sulk behind the scarlet pale of cities** through the door in-walks **(and that's why they are called monstrosities)** Sir the Philosopher. **and die forever without soul or meter,** Philosophy and rhetoric, they **propounding and redounding on each issue.** whack each other **That's why the cities too are called the cities.** hard over issues of **They're crying out for attitude and rhyme!** ethics in the oratory art. **Man, if you have an attitude, then don it,** Rhetoric and philosophy **and then everything else becomes a sonnet.** slam each other plum in the head, skull and slats all o'er the auditorium. & on the chance that this occasion is being closely monitored, I'd add deconstruction, it's also quite good. Herr Doktor, lieber Frau, deconstruct me now!

One Sensation, Two Sensation

Most folks think it is an easy living— hunting for dratted stories the way we do. As if we were in this just for the money & for the basic do-nothingism rather than for truth. What smart a critique! **The lightbulb's legal splendor, gasping, laps** We are not in them **at muted promises of higher station;** movies, folks. Hollywood's **the lisping crispness of its tungsten wisp** not cutting us all a huge **aspires to a brief whitehot contemplation** cushy monthly "check" **of jobs well done. The capo rubs his hands,** plus per diem. & no-**pleased at how paper holds the paperweight;** thing at all could be **the bubbly foams; the outfit too expands.** further from the truth, as **But his cheroot outshines his young friend's fate.** a matter of fact, **The check's a clever ruse, capisce? Cashed in,** than such a faulty **unlike the kid himself, it'll never be.** assumption. We're reporters, **At Carpe Diem, philosophically,** so what do we do? We distribute **a friend will plug the sucker in the brain** to people InForMatIOn. **tonight. Oozing the milk of kindness home,** We are analysts, what **the capo signs the check, knowing the system.** do we do? We turn raw, formless data into intelligible InForMatIOn. Yeah, it sells, so? Feel free to consult further pages at a small (reasonable) premium. Send all inquiries with check/money order to our customer service.

I'll Write

I'm 12 and it's summer. I can't read today: Esenin's verse falls asleep in my lap, in spite of words like prostitutes, scandal, hooligan, suicide. The water will soon be too cold **Flag down a wind shiny with lightning spooks.** for swims. **The skies find their unquestionable never.** The deer has **When seen from deep within, windows are books** peed in **systematically perused by the clever.** the lake, say locals: **Goldenrod denies ever being born.** their codename for this **The botanist on his straw train toots his horn** switch of **into the semi-desert beyond the horizon,** season. For me **whose dust offers nothing to clamp eyes on** it soon will be **but an attenuated haloxylon or saxaul.** ciao to Strokino, **We are of the same school** end of vacation, back to town. **and rattle on to meet another challenge** Should I hide in **with our keen art. The night, a subtle ruse,** the woods, **etches itself in us while it eschews** knowing every trunk, **all fixity in its poorly settled range.** path and swamp? Feed on raw russulas? I think of survival in winter. Good grief. What right have they to drag me away from here, from her? I will write her, she'll never write back, but I'll write her.

Coastwise Lights

law window wallet egg library bulk chalice zing ten doe tin reduction op warper throe tin foil table plaintiff mind task rye *A slow evening walk.* twig surf star *Pale and abstract lips* skittles *pretend no understanding* street zebra roe *of this melancholy.* ducttape torch horde wad dog El air drawee factor *The castanea dentata* lycra swig stock *is thick on the air,* nexus cottage *that disturbing odor* pellet nappy *all down the boulevard.* bullet catnip plush tentacle cornice wardrobe manner *Who knows why,* pluggist carp *transient as geraniums,* bidder *a mind sleeps on a restaurant* locust eel *doily with deep abandon?* master fish preponderance thigh lather hiccup toe *The moon is on the ocean* lilt television *sands. Coastwise lights* jug ply *play dizzy tricks with foghorns.* orchestra *My shadow has four hands.* disagreement flop Jose Antarctica rain piggy *Hurrah for the harbor seagulls* pliers soil *on isles and lobster buoys,* turnip sip *the night's spindrift blood* sea matter lip *against the absent stars.* locomotion zone refrigerator serenity partridge butt flip woo ticket speculum whisker winter ore she sole ewe timer

Suburbi Et Suborbi

The loveliest of trees, the loquat hangs with ripened loquats prepending a house wall in the land of Redwood City's ultra-post-hyper-suburbia. Ying and yang, yum and yuck, all in one. A million dollar house stands *Our life comes to us as a big surprise.* **high (ouch) in similar neighborhood,** *The world sublimely penetrates our eyes.* **for are we not all known by our** *All things combined, the brain seems mighty fine.* **neighbors, the self being** *But folks, why are your shoulders next to mine,* **the differential effect of** *why is my purpose to your purpose next?* **of business relations. In this our** *You aren't content to know that I am "text"* **age, repost form data is instant.** *but think we tread across the same sunrays* **Easy submit beta, and no wish** *and drizzle that fill the collective gaze,* **now to attempt, in claws, ink laws,** *under whose wet paw may the heart unwelt* **a brand-new misanthropy. It has** *and all indifference to passion melt.* **builded itself a niche on the horizon,** *And truly everything'll be melting soon.* **zoomed in via a hypnotic gloom,** *Jupiter's moons are junipers in June,* **metal propel metal, ledge end gone** *and what's July but something that transcends* **awol. But the cadet school** *the opaque boundaries among friends?* **of stark abnormalcy has announced its admissions to mastermind fresh eremitic earlobes, celestial scooters wheeling crayon sundown, sad myrtle for the next tribe. Is it not time for tiny bye-bye, taken apart, severed to the dim pieces, to molecules of sleep?**

Recollections

The bridge knits its temptations to the raw max. We lumber. Nary a moment and plonk, we are here. Welcome to the thereafter, the aftertear, the preherein, the evernow. Here we offer *Love's documented story will be told* **each other drinks with winks** *as Courier 14 bold continues to unfold* **on the dacha verandah** *across my email emacs to where gestures* **among the stars alone** *of jonquils in your cobalt vase are dim.* **(and what, is this Russia?),** *Their hubris hides behind no pseudonym,* **smoking cheapo cigs,** *but their reflection ripples with suggestions* **filterless, unloading** *of older screens and dustier than this,* **a basket of freshly collected** *on quite another continent. The flowers* **russulas, chanterelles, &** *where lilacs then, our leisured followers.* **liter of dry white wine.** *I'll bet you that the shrub we robbed still lives,* **What, Feteasca,** *wish I could write to it and ask what gives,* **whose vine brims with** *but I am no epistolary apprentice.* **suns of Moldovan soil? Let's** *In memory, the loveliest of sieves,* **pull off our boots by candlelight,** *may tender life forever twine with leaves.* **we are dead beat, we two have trodden cattycorner across the vineyard you say reminds you of a flock of crows, jogged over gravel, exercising youthful ambiguities, with countless miles to go till we hit Amherst, Mass.**

To Assuage

As I and the instrument adapt to each other, its chromatic temperings because of & notwithstanding (perhaps rather *What was that note? I do not know,* more notwithstanding *I don't have perfect pitch.* than because of), I ain't well- *I still have two more years to go* tempered yet, but ah well, *to know without a glitch* what's that to whom. All I want is to sing. A voice can penetrate the innermost lugubrious *my re from do* depths, covey a dark vision. For instance, *(which tone is which),* I could sing into the phone to the *but man I really wanna know,* tune of the busy signal. Just *so I indulge this itch. be* the signal, the B flat. Neighbors would think I'm phone phreaking. Or be the elevator tone, *Into the bargain, I have made* an E. But that's always *a very stupid bet* between me and the instrument. Or sing *that I will ram into my head* the logically obvious, or at *the 88 key set* any arte everything that is logically obvious to a non-totally-oblivious mind. Strict rules of entailment *at my quite venerable age,* in analytic truth, as well as in *do re mi fa so la ti,* empirical causality inductively derived, *if only merely to assuage* the ailment of unyouth, the paying *this sad mortality.* off of its ticket at destination. Or sing the ironclad mortality of the moral agent, the sad inactivity of his will, funicular grief with its looking downward from the sky.

States of Affairs

Hatching out of the train, we stretch our legs and suddenly blend with the scenery. In one stride the milfoils leap underfoot and we walk beyond the the railroad into the green mortality of the woods, hardly knowing what **Two solitary dogs in all the park** *lures us, why. Twigs crackle with our* **seek out each other with a knowing bark.** *progress through cobwebs on* **The poet on the curbside feels expended.** *law-abiding junipers. Questions* **Meanwhile the day continues open-ended,** *spin out of them. Wild forest* **the sun persists in wrapping glowing wool** *growlers in the underbrush* **over eyes of the Ringe and Latin School.** *can hear them. Which lichens* **Cops drift by with a vigilant assurance,** *become which environment?* **ideas of order permeate their neurons.** *Which treetop is this cheeriole's* **The athlete walks back from his sweaty run.** *meaning? We transfer our* **His carbobottle finds the garbage can.** *attentions to the lake, lost in windy* **The flower lady hastens to her roses.** *paroxysms of bulrush, then back.* **Dim consequences stem from upfront causes,** *Honey agarics in their thin-* **and in their self-perpetuating race** *legged millions besiege stumps that* **reflective shadows play on every face.** *rear their rears. The hornet flies freely over the odd berry. St. John's wort blooms in appropriate locations, admiring how the bank loops back upon itself on a small island, all pines and pines and reflections of pines. There is nothing but temporary clarity.*

A Silence within a Silence

Into a mad-locked heart blood bellows fresh hurrah;
witch-hazel whispers' lamps hang in a lonely air.
Never before have nights been quite so traffic-free,
The subtle bendings of a creed *with the cicada's code*
in moments overcome by greed, *never as clear as this.*
proverbial twitchings of the rear *Ardent with bombs of*
in moments overcome by fear, *blush, blindfold in leafy*
the shallow moneys in our dreams *dew, witchcrafts on*
for mellow honeys of our creams *prickly stems arch*
collected into fulgent hives *across august hours. Moths*
through banking systems of our lives, *of forgiveness trip*
rapacious fantasies of whoredom *over my wine and lip,*
in moments overcome by boredom, *your silky eyebrow,*
incanting +I was a late bloomer+ *our hubris, laughter,*
in moments overcome by humor, *despair slowly as one*
cosmic contempt for private breath *by one once, then*
in moments overcome by death. *once again and then*
once again once again sounds and their sounds depart
netted in flapping flight drowned in a keyhole's well
crowned with a dog-bit moon up by the earth-lit cloud.

Simple Joys of Food & Drink

My zinging zinfandel, self-raised, dead-eye refined, *Speaking on behalf of the wooden spatula,* **well "off of"** *how are you today, my lady the arugula?* **the tall divine,** *May I inquire after the roast beef,* **wherewith I thus** *a sandwich of suspended disbelief?* **here stand baffled.** *Could I address through a tangle of sprouts* **In my sick** *the honey dijon mustard and mayonnaise?* **head where** *Ought I to apply a leaflet of lettuce* **flotsam jets / jetsam** *over the three round slices of tomatoes?* **floats, there's** *Yes, you may introduce me, if you insist,* **need for your** *to a few sweet roasted peppers, please.* **action as blue-** *But don't disturb the cheeses, let them sleep:* **green algae** *cheeses have other promises to keep.* **(cyanobacterium)** *Spread it all out upon my favorite grain* **of inspiration** *in its loaf of auburn love at Au Bon Pain.* **call for drops of drink, bits of booze. Until we die we may as well enjoy, what the hell, for we decay or prosper as we choose. Come, darling, let's get drunk on zinfandel.**

Letters from the Past

Sorry to have been of late been such a lousy correspondent — in a flat spin all the time, it has been inexpressibly difficult to keep the act organized amid the vortex of stuff I have been finding myself **Never again** involved in in the recent past. Teaching now over, I'm **will clever leguminous clover** somewhat more flexible with my **lisp its refrain** energies & priorities; so here's finally a hello. How **to the scythe of a luminous mower,** y'all doin'? How's Moscow? **not over admirable, but a lover** Seriously, there's been too much **to rays of a sunset sun.** Fogg over the Atlantic; kind of hard for **Not all things begun** us to see through to each other clearly, no? **are yet totally over,** So tell me all about it. Meanwhile I'll briefly **but have you wondered how long it must** fill you in on us. From **take until the last rhyme is denied access,** a long, underdeveloped, **is absolutely deleted? Indeed,** analytically hypercorrect, wet chilly **until the coiling millipede of dust** spring (due to which, 10 O'Clock **encroaches here with its nine-millionth tarsus,** News informs us, **chasing in vain a starlit tumbleweed.** entomologists predict on our coast an inordinate transcendence of mosquitoes) and into summer. Longfellow House perks its chimneys up. All night I entertained the wildlife in the two squares, the stars honeydew melons in lazulite.

Indian Summer

The troubled fountain pen knows less about our grief
than about laughter, but tarries when a yellow leaf
twentieth century art gives *slides to its sweet thereafter,*
us existentialism and jazz *not caring one whit for and*
the new encyclopedia says *losing torn sight of us and*
though I forget which page it is *ours. We've come out*
modernism and postmodernism *to notice and discuss*
and fascist art and communist *September's warm strip-*
eternal turnings of the wheel *tease on the city, eyeing*
eternal hurtings of the real *citizens and aliens in TGIF*
unwinding, impermanent residents of time, drifting
across life with patience, all held together by gravity.

Modulo Feeling

What you need to open is a new file. Call it a feel for life. My father and I used to talk about artificial intelligence a lot, which was his specialty, as I was growing up. For example, you can have a program that will make the computer write something really wild. Because when it is writing, there is like a cathode that connects with the computer's brain, and there swerve rivers far past recognition, and likelihood's butterflies are already settling in the nearness of our gaze, and this means the river will be an opening, disburthened of its erstwhile behavior, but still dynamic. And that means we're already in March, and soon is my birthday. I am no longer sure how old I am then. The telegraph wires are tall, and altogether elsewhere my wet blue school uniform is hung on a wire to dry, and Tom barks on the balcony in the rain. Tomik, back to the balcony, says Mom. Was a mongrel, maternally a Spaniel and paternally a mutt. A big box of apples and a lizard in a big glass jar behind it, live tarantulas in other jars, a grafted cactus, and Twits the canary on my head (who later flew away). Me a budding biologist, but language a distraction. You see, the idea is that something counts as "artificial intelligence" so long as you can't distinguish between a program's thought process and a human's thought process. You can't tell whether you're talking to a human, or by reading its writing. Because when it is writing, there's like spiral stairway at the institute, and the colleagues have gone out for a smoke, but you are stuck with your algorithm, worried about funds for the project, your boss a bastard non-entity. The question of Intelligence Itself is, in the Platonic sense, never answered, but we are working out what's intelligence as we know it, that which keeps us from drifting rudderless in a sea of ill luck. Piles of dictionary entries on punched cards and various thesauri. Too must be confirmed. Isn't copyrighted. Thus, to answer your question, yes, poetry too. As you can see on the graph, computers can prospectively write it very well. Not necessarily wild stuff. Fine, measured stuff, with taste, as if direct from experience. They, for example, will be able to write lyric poetry, you'll understand when you grow up. Because when it is writing, there is like a modulo feeling, and it begins to multiply itself further and further, until the heart becomes incompatible with the brain, and then absolute intelligence is detached, as the hypothesis states, into an outer darkness. What happens to it thence we do not know.

Litmus Test

Didn't want to go to the damn party in the first place,
needed to "catch a lecture" the next morning
on Renaissance Florence, one of those stupid 9-a.m.-on-Saturday
events, but my buddy insisted sangria, perfect chance to chat
up Jessica and Jake, so we went
at midnight. Sangria my ass. I mean it tasted extra nice,
bootilicious, but they'd run out of ice
and Jessica and Jake had already left. Half an hour later
three spluttering purple volcanoes
of indeterminate size, but perfectly harmless and hospitable,
spun winking out of the texture of the tabletop,
pouring forth an interminable wordlist full of words
into pulsating Buddha-faced saucers. My armchair
floated in the breeze over the seaweed-infested carpet
dead to rights. I was chary of wading through its Dead Sea
waters, though I needed to pee. My buddy goes man,
I think we just drank some acid, should've
poured the stuff that's on the table but I wanted it cold
from the fridge cuz they've no ice
so anyway we can always and later too you know
all that, now best stay where you are, best to just to hang in look
I know you have to pee "like ouch" but listen
I've been thinking this week all week every day
for three years now, it's driving me nuts I've always
wanted to talk you up about how you know sometimes
that feeling that we call sublime or subliminal whichever
you can also feel it right that wholesome feeling
a bird tipping from branch to branch to branch in luminous light
a bee crawling from bract to bract a strange kind of lyric feeling
the inexpressible what we felt in childhood
is really what we're all about like they're cluing you in on it now
gluing suing slewing you in on it. Spack,
a strange music turned itself on and wouldn't quit,
that bizarre non-quitter music. Anyway when they sang
happy birthday dear Humphrey

at 2 a.m. I needed to pee especially badly
and trudged off through the interminable apartment
though my buddy hadn't yet finalized his discourse.
I'd never been in a non-finite apartment before,
after 27 rooms I stopped counting
because I almost wet my pants before finding the bathroom
plus had to wait another ten minutes
while someone was getting sick in there.
And finally when I felt I was going back to normal
and washing my hands, I saw in the mirror,
which was in the key of E flat minor,
myself as a winged demon with golden horns on top
and colored rotating spirals for my pupils, my stare
expressive of the universal doom.
Then there was a descent down the three-mile jade
staircase and gigantic escalades of diamond snow.
My buddy and I sat to our heart's content on steaming grilles
in the pavement by the Store 24 warming ourselves
(though in fact it was hot) with other nocturnal characters,
who thankfully seemed to know no English, and in the end
I realized that we are chemical through and through,
so determinate and so chemical, while sliding in crystal insects up
the conic mountain of spacetime, with its mass but no weight,
pure composition. Soon by the creaking of refreshed pedestrians
I opened up to the idea that there was one hour left until the lecture.
Is supermarket coffee inherently such a palette of taste,
or was it the radically contingent chemistry of my palate
that temporarily made it so? My buddy had left to sleep it off
(wish I had his worries), but I tried to recompose alone
the ordinary coherency of life. All I heard were the dubious
reverberations of a mid-90s train passing underground.
Savonarola's sermon, to which I had eventually made it
across the Alps, focused on the ideals of asceticism, poverty
and visionary piety. His project of a bohemian republic
appealed to me deeply as I took faithful notes

diagonally across my notebook (which was unliftable).
Fellow aspirants peeked at me inquisitorially,
but I waved them off, staring at the preacher's
skinny jowl, enormous nose, dark cowl in profile. Then
I had nothing left or planned for the rest of Saturday
except to get home to my two-bit moth-devoured
studio with its many topological holes
and zip up my brain. I stepped across some literature
to my solitary bed, dedicated exclusively to the twin purposes
of study and sleep, and elongated myself as best I could.
Sleep was out of the question, issues of the irreducible
multiplicity pressing harshly upon my overburdened lobes.
I yearned to be one, complete, so I arched and reached
for the telephone. Yes, dropped some acid last night
first time ever, haven't slept. Please come save me,
I hate acid. You hadn't slept much since New York either,
but you arrived instantly, as if wading through atrocious snow
came as naturally to you as levitation to a saint.
I laughed suddenly, for the first time in a month,
shocked to discover your red hair had its usual color.
You had American Spirit cigarettes (I was out),
and in minutes we stood at the foot of Lee Bo's Cantonese Kitchen,
whose second floor seemed unreachable on foot.
I sighed with relief in the pentatonic elevator.
In the bathroom things went well this time,
no dragons in the mirror. You fed me with a spoon,
then with chopsticks. The hot and sour soup
was indeed hot and sour, it counteracted my internal chill,
and the salt jumbo shrimp were verily salty and jumbo.
The green tea you poured into me sip by tiny sip
made me realize for the first time
how perfect we were for each other. I wept like a whale.
You had changed my chemical composition forever.

God, empowered to the max,
from this world that I have lost
break my crux and ancient crest,
cake me with the dust of toast,

eat me with a side of jam
into that far cloudy home
where I too am what I am,
have become what I've become.

A Life, in 500 Words or Less

word time thing look
number sound people
water call side
work part place round
year show name form
sentence help line turn
cause move right play
home hand port spell
land change light kind
need house picture
animal point
mother world earth
father head stand
page country answer
school study plant
cover food state
thought city tree
cross farm start story
press night life walk
example ease
paper group music
letter mile river
care second book
science room friend
idea fish mountain
stop base horse color
face wood plain girl
list bird body
family song
measure door product
class wind question
ship area rock
order fire problem
piece pass king space
hour step ground interest

verb table morning
vowel pattern center
love person money
road rain rule cold
notice voice unit
power town leader
machine note plan
figure star noun
field pound beauty
drive week ocean
minute mind tail
fact street inch nothing
course wheel force object
surface moon island
foot system test
record boat gold plane
stead wonder laugh check
game shape heat snow
tire paint language
ball wave drop heart
present dance engine
position material
size weight general
matter circle pair
syllable pick count
square reason length
subject region energy
hunt brother ride cell
fraction forest race
window store summer
train sleep exercise
wall wish board winter
instrument glass grass
edge sign visit past
weather month bear

hope flower jump baby
village root raise metal
push paragraph hair cook
powder floor result
hill safe century coast
copy phrase sand soil
roll temperature finger
industry value fight beat
view sense case lake moment
scale spring child consonant
nation dictionary
milk speed method
organ section dress cloud
surprise stone design experiment
bottom iron flat skin smile
crease hole trade melody
trip office mouth
symbol trouble seed
tone joint break lady
yard rise blood touch
cent team wire cost garden
flow fair bank control
woman man captain
practice doctor noon
ring character insect
period radio atom
human history effect
element student corner
party supply bone rail
capital chair danger
fruit soldier process guess
wing neighbor crowd corn
poem string bell meat tube
dollar stream fear sight triangle
planet hurry boss colony clock

mine major search print spot
desert suit rose block chart
art success company
event deal term wife shoe
shoulder camp cotton
nine truck noise level
chance shop throw property
column molecule salt
nose anger claim continent
oxygen sugar death skill season
solution magnet silver branch
match suffix sister steel guide
experience score apple pitch
coat mass card band rope
slip dream evening condition
feed tool smell valley seat
master track parent shore
division sheet substance favor
chord original share station
bread charge offer segment
slave duck market degree
chick dear enemy reply drink
support speech nature range
steam motion path liquid
quotient shell neck mail sport
husband mall network television
movie car driver aunt uncle
meal diner lunch program schedule
award competition stock computer
teacher pool kid spoon fork knife
asset hospital insurance eye
arm leg salary fee challenge

Earth

But what to make of the diminished lot,
of what man could have got and yet has not?
But let him simply while away the day,
and soon this will not matter anyway.
Walking in vain across a cloudy sky,
he scans the grasslands with an acid eye,
like a slightly more modern Robert Frost.
But what of what man had yet somehow lost?
Staring at nature helps him to forget,
to come to terms, to cancel out the debt.
All night he whistled with a mockingbird
and now on his old keyboard types a word
or two into the world and falls asleep.
The land has willows, something needs to weep.

Printed in the United States
65765LVS00002B/1-219